TAN

Prison Scene.

Hostage in Afghanistan

Peter Collister

Pentland Press Ltd
Edinburgh · Cambridge · Durham · USA

First published in 1999 by
The Pentland Press Ltd.
1 Hutton Close
South Church
Bishop Auckland
Durham

British Library Cataloguing in Publication Data.
A catalogue record for this book is available
from the British Library.

ISBN 1 85821 636 2

Typeset by George Wishart & Associates, Whitley Bay.
Printed and bound by Antony Rowe Ltd., Chippenham.

Contents

Illustrations

Maps

Preface

For readers unfamiliar with the history of the British in India it may be useful to have a very brief summary of what had gone before. During the seventeenth century the East India Company established trading posts on the west and east coasts by permission of the Moghul Emperors, Muslim conquerors of a mainly Hindu sub-continent. As the Empire disintegrated, so the Company's trading centres expanded and took over administration of sometimes lawless areas on their borders. Later came wars with the French and with Indian rulers, now virtually independent of the Emperors. By the 1830s the Company was ruling most of Bengal and large areas of hinterland behind Bombay and Madras, in three separate 'Presidencies', each with its own Governor, although Bengal's Governor-General was supreme. They also each had their own armies whose officers, appointed to the Company's regiments, always rated junior to those of similar rank in the royal regiments and were sometimes from a different and more impecunious social background (General Nott, whose force advanced from Kandahar during the last stages of the hostages' ordeal, was a case in point).

Although the East India Company continued to rule large parts of India until 1858, a year after the start of the Indian mutiny (called the 1st War of Independence or the Great Rebellion by some Indian historians, although it was largely a military revolt confined almost entirely to the Bengal army) nevertheless, the British Government at home exercised a controlling political interest. At this period Russia was expanding southwards into Muslim central Asia (into the lands now once again becoming independent) and there was a good deal of espionage carried out by British and Russian officers in the disputed territories, and jockeying for favour with the ruling Khans.

The people who form the subject matter of this book were

mainly British officers in the service of the Company, several of whom had taken part in the 'Great Game' as this war of espionage came to be called. They and their wives had a background of familiarity with the Indian sub-continent where they had lived in a style very different from their circumstances as hostages. Others, including the two disastrous commanders, Elphinstone and Shelton, were from royal regiments and had served in other parts of the world as well as India.

They were, on the whole, fairly well-educated people but their spelling, especially of Afghan and Indian names, was rather bizarre and I have adopted, except when quoting, the Anglicised versions of most contemporary writing.

Finally, the reader might justifiably wonder, as this is avowedly not a military history of the war, but is a description of how these people reacted to a hostage situation, why nearly half the book is taken up by other matters, including the Afghan background, the occupation and the retreat. This is because it is all germane to the main theme, that the hostage reactions cannot really be studied without some knowledge of what had gone before and the roles that some of the hostages had played in the preceding period. There is also a last section devoted to their subsequent lives, some of which may have been deeply affected by the traumas of their captivity.

Introduction

The brooding heights of Afghanistan have seen many a conquering army arrive in martial splendour, only to return across the forbidding passes in straggling disarray: from Alexander and his Greeks to Tamurlane; from Mahmoud of Ghazni to the Emperor Babur who left his bones near Kabul; and the Russians in our own day. Yet none of these suffered a fate more fearsome than that of the British/Indian force of 5,000 men and three times that number of camp followers, servants, women and children in the bleak winter of 1841-2 when only one man reached their objective at Jelalabad, a mere thirty miles away, and only a few others, wounded and in hiding, lived to tell the tale. It was like a Greek tragedy foreordained from the beginning by the characters of the British commanders and their political masters and the nature of their Afghan opponents. It is a tale told often before and is not the main subject of this book, to which it forms the preamble.

The modern world is all too familiar with the taking of hostages but few people realize that the concept of hostage-taking is not new. Indigenous armies as well as invaders, fighting across the Indian sub-continent in Moghul times and before, used to do it and it was not uncommon for the sons of a prince to be freely offered as surety; and the tribal chiefs of the central Asian Khanates and of Afghanistan did it after raiding the forts of their rivals. Quite often the hostages would be held under tolerable conditions and would be returned when the political situation had improved. Not so in the modern world where the so-called hostages are held as prisoners on the assumption that their countries of origin would encourage certain political actions. Of the hostages in Afghanistan in 1841-2, some had been offered up voluntarily by the British after the initial Afghan request had been made but most ended up as prisoners, the raison d'être of the original hostage-taking long since forgotten. The British had entered the country in 1839 to replace on the throne a ruler whom the British considered would be more favourable towards them than his rival in the diplomatic war with Russia, whose central Asian conquests were creeping southward towards Afghanistan. A British/Indian army of over 20,000 entered the country, fought a number of battles and occupied the capital, Kabul, before settling down to a congenial life in cantonments. During the year of 1841 they felt so secure that they were able to reduce their strength drastically, sending large numbers back to India, whilst those that were left built houses, sent for wives and families, created a racecourse and indulged in all kinds of sport, enjoyed almost as much by some of the Afghans, with whom the officers established social relationships. All the time there were signs of disaffection spotted only by more perceptive young army officers seconded to political posts. There were many causes for this, quite apart from the inhabitants' natural distaste for any occupying force. Even the British began to realize that their replacement king was a poor substitute for his predecessor. The man in the bazaar was resentful of the great rise in prices as a result of shopkeepers putting them up for the British; and Afghans of all classes resented the free use of their women made by British officers and soldiers.

By the end of 1841 the general disaffection felt by Afghans towards their imposed sovereign and his British masters resulted in an uprising, the upshot of which, due in large part to the incredible stupidity of the British military chiefs, was that the army (so called, but by then little more than a brigade and less than a division) was forced into a treaty situation, agreeing to withdraw whilst leaving a few British officers behind as hostages, as a guarantee against treaty violation, who were to be released when the force returned to India. In return a number of Afghan chiefs undertook to ensure the army's safe withdrawal, which, in the event they were unable or unwilling to do because of the fractured nature of Afghan society and the refusal of the Ghilzai chieftains to accept any treaty obligation. In the end a combination of appalling winter weather and raids by tribesmen ensured the decimation of the British force.

Meanwhile the few officer hostages had been joined by others, together with their wives and families who, it was thought, would stand a better chance of survival in the hands of the leading chiefs than staying with the army – correctly, as it transpired. Later, their numbers were augmented by wounded soldiers and officers picked up on the fields of battle, so that the number released nine months later was well over a hundred, all of whom by then regarded themselves as prisoners rather than hostages. During that time they endured considerable hardships, being marched from place to place, although admittedly the ladies usually rode on camel-drawn conveyances and some of the officers had horses. Even so, their ultimate delivery was always in doubt, given the unpredictable and volatile nature of their chief captor, Mohammed Akbar Khan, son of the deposed Dost Mohammed, himself by then in comfortable British-imposed exile in northern India.

The hostages suffered at times physical hardship as great as any hostages in the modern world and their lives and destinations were equally uncertain but most of the time certain civilities were retained and the relationship between hostages and captors was not one of unmitigated hostility on both sides; rather, a grudging admiration was accorded by some of the hostages, without losing sight of Akbar's well-merited reputation for ferocity. Nor, despite the courtesy with which he treated them, did they forget their value to him for ransom or sale as slaves at Bokhara and Khiva to the north of Afghanistan where they would join the hundreds of Russian slaves captured by Turcoman raiders during the Russian advance to the south.

In particular, the relationships between the few military officers who had held political appointments, attached to the army on account of their linguistic and diplomatic skills, and were able to converse with their captors in Persian, and their jailers is fascinating as it unfolds in the diaries and memoirs of several of the hostages. Akbar not only referred to them as his 'guests' (an all too familiar phrase) but seemed at times even to mean it, protecting them from marauding tribesmen – for even his writ was not law in a land of tribal loyalties – and, within the confines of their existence, trying to make them comfortable as far as was within his power. The few British officers who got to know him well learnt to have a wary respect for him.

The story of the hostages is not only interesting for its contrasts and similarities with events of recent times, but also for the light it sheds on the social structures of both races at that time. They shared attitudes towards the manly virtues of courage, chivalry and loyalty; and although they might not have admitted it their attitude towards women was not dissimilar. The British put women on a pedestal – hence the bloodthirsty revenge after the Cawnpore massacre seventeen years later – but with few exceptions (such as Henry and Honoria Lawrence) they did not make friends of them. Although his wife shared his captivity Lieutenant Vincent Eyre never once mentioned her in his diary. For their part the Afghans greatly prized their women and sprang to their defence when threatened but lasting friendships were with men. Resentment of their husbands' homosexual relationships appears to have been one of the reasons why a number of Afghan women gave themselves to the British.

Just as there was all the difference in the world between Akbar's band of chiefs and the bloodthirsty Ghilzai tribesmen who, on several occasions came near to annihilating the hostages had it not been for Akbar's men, or between them and the Kuzzilbash people who were ultimately responsible for the hostages' relief, so were there marked differences within the British group where the social gradations of nineteenth-century Britain were never obliterated. The few soldiers' wives, 'the women', were usually lodged separately from the officers' ladies, however crude the quarters, and the soldiers' accommodation was inferior to that of the officers who, like Akbar himself, paid great respect to Lady MacNaghten, widow of the murdered Envoy, and the indomitable Lady Sale who cared not a fig for any of them and voiced her trenchant criticisms not only of the Afghans but also of her countrymen. Wife of the general commanding at Jelalabad, she should have been a general herself. There would have been no retreat in that case – but that is anticipating what is to come.

This is a story, remarkably familiar in some ways, of Europeans held hostage in a Muslim country, whose religion, ways of life, values and attitudes towards the sanctity of human life, clashed with their own. It is a story of privation, fear, sudden death, the ravages of disease, of the uncertainty of fate, of strange cross currents of affinities between captors and captives, in which the heroes and the villains were to be found on both sides, which each had their share of cowardice, treachery and heroism.

During their nine months captivity some of the hostages kept diaries, notably Lieutenant Eyre and Captain Johnson. Others, particularly Lady Sale, wrote letters describing their experiences which found their way the mere thirty miles to the British lines at Jelalabad; and others, including Captains Lawrence and Mackenzie wrote reminiscences in later life. All these sources have been used and to a large extent the actors in this drama have been allowed to speak with their own voices. Some, whose writings would have been particularly helpful such as Captains Conolly and Troup, were victims of disease and others, notably Major Pottinger, died shortly afterwards. Most of them, however, have left no record: the soldiers and their wives, the four children born in captivity and the others who experienced it, returned to lives of obscurity and, it is to be hoped, to domestic comfort in their own land, although few will ever have forgotten the nine months when they were hostage in Afghanistan.

CHAPTER I

Afghanistan in the Nineteenth Century

Afghanistan covers an area of about 50,000 square miles, bounded to the north by the river Oxus, beyond which is the former USSR, although 150 years ago the Russian borders were far to the north before steadily expanding southwards during the century at the expense of the independent kingdom of Khiva and Bokhara. Afghanistan is about 700 miles from the north-east to the south-west and 600 miles from Herat and the Iranian frontier to the Khyber pass. The centre of the country includes part of the Hindu Kush range of mountains which lead down to lesser hills and plains. Its mountainous borders include a number of passes, used not only by invaders but also by trading caravans to and from India, Persia and China.

In the nineteenth century Herat province was very important, touching the eastern border of Persia, of which it was at various times an integral part, frequently being claimed by both sides. The roads to Herat converged from all areas: from the Caspian, from Merv and Bokhara, and from India via Kandahar, a place of great strategic importance between two rivers on a well-cultivated plain. The city of Kandahar was strongly walled with double bastions and had wide tree-lined streets. From there, Indian merchants imported silk, leather and metals into further parts of the country, and exported to India and beyond, camels' wool, horses, tobacco, preserved fruits and drugs. It has a good climate in winter but is hellish hot in summer, the heat beating off from the sandhills all around. West of Kandahar is Seistan, part of which is now in Iran, a wide area drained by the Hunan lake. It is on the borders of Afghanistan, Persia and Baluchistan and in the last century depended largely on irrigation canals constructed before the Persian occupation.

Kabul lies between mountains which bisect Kabul province as does the Kabul river. It was a meeting place of many races, from Turkestan and Kafriristan as well as Tajiks, Pushtoons and many others. In the nineteenth century it was a thriving city with a productive hinterland growing wheat and barley. It was famous for its enormous bazaar, destroyed by the British 'Army of Revenge' in 1842. It also had some fine buildings, notably the Bala Hissar, the great citadel and home of the country's rulers. Butkah district was the most developed in those days and grew quantities of fruit. In the summer much of the population lived in tents, trading camels, mules, horses and cattle to Turkestan, India and Khorassan.

In the north-east there are mountain ranges and deep valleys, and in those days there was little agriculture; however, it is rich in mineral resources and forests. Afghan Turkestan rivalled Herat and Kandahar in importance, with caravans going to and from Bokhara and India. Fifty miles to the west was Balkh consisting in those days mainly of the ruins of earlier civilisations. Finally there was Jelalabad, which will figure largely in this story. At a lower altitude than most other places in Afghanistan it is set in a fertile countryside.

Above all therefore, Afghanistan is a land of contrasts and by no means fits the popular concept of a country consisting only of barren mountains and ferocious inhabitants. This can be seen in the observations of the hostages who, despite their predicament, at times waxed lyrical about the lush green meadows watered by clear flowing streams, the abundance of wild flowers, the bird-song and the fertile crops. At other times they were overawed by the awful majesty of the stark serrated mountains, the precipitous ascents and descents they had to trudge, when even the ladies had to dismount and walk, the narrow, forbidding passes and hostile defiles.

The climate offers almost as many contrasts as the geography. Although in most parts the winters are cold but sunny and the summers scorching hot, with annual rainfall of only ten inches, there are great variations. The hostages rarely mentioned rain in their diaries and memoirs although they did experience several earthquakes and extremes of heat and cold.

No wonder that such a variegated country, with its enormous natural barriers and hazards, had produced by the early nineteenth century, before the construction of modern roads and the coming of the internal combustion engine, a fragmented populace where every mountain and valley had its own chieftains, living in square, forbidding forts, such as the many in which the hostages were housed. Every tribe had its own enemies and the concept of a national state was still so novel that it was often disregarded; and the natural form of succession to kingship was still assassination.

The Greek historian Ptolemy had referred to the country between Baluchistan in the south and the Hindu Kush to the north, as Ariana (the name adopted by the national airline) but for centuries the inhabitants thought of themselves first and foremost as Pushtoons, Ghilzais, Kuzzilbash, Duranis and many other tribal names. Alexander, who conquered Kabul, Kandahar and Ghazni brought with him Greek colonists and garrisons who, after he and his beautiful Roxana had departed, stayed on under his Seleucid successors who were expelled by the hordes from central Asia. In the course of time there were the Buddhists who left behind their wonderful statuary at Gandara, now in Pakistan, with its strong Grecian influence, and huge statues in Afghanistan, as well as Hindus, Arabs, Persians and Turks in various parts of the country. The Islamic conquerors brought their religion, to which the Afghans have been faithful ever since. One of the greatest was Mahmoud of Ghazni (988-1030) whose Empire included most of Afghanistan, trans-Oxiana in northern India, the Punjab and part of Persia but his capital was at Ghazni where he founded a university.

Genghis Khan, the Mongols and their descendants ruled until the Seljuk Turks under the great Tamurlane subdued the country on the way to sack Delhi. When he died his Empire disintegrated but his descendants continued to rule in Herat, Balksh, Ghazni, Kabul and Kandahar. One of them was Babur, ruler of Badekhshan, Kabul and Kandahar. He invaded India where he founded the great empire of the Moghuls that was to last for well over 200 years. It was so long before he returned to Afghanistan that the Uzbegs had taken Badekshash and the Persians Herat and Kandahar, only Ghazni and Kabul province remaining in Moghul hands.

In the early eighteenth century, when the Ghilzais of Kandahar threw out the Persians and the Duranis took Herat, a state of Afghanistan began to emerge and a king, Ahmed Khan was chosen by the Pushtoon. He organized it on Persian lines and governed as first among equals, favouring his own clan, the Abdalis, who changed their name to Durani ('of the pearls'). His predecessor, Nadir Shah had conquered the whole country before invading India and sacking Delhi but had been assassinated on his way home laden with loot. His successor, Ahmed Shah, his general, took over and ruled until 1777 when he too was assassinated. He had founded the Durani empire, including the whole of modern Afghanistan, Baluchistan, parts of Persia, Sind, Derajat and the Punjab as far as Lahore. After him, under his son Timur, the empire began to decline and under his grandson Zaman, the Punjab was overrun by the Sikhs. There were family conflicts until in 1803 the throne passed, as a result of a plot,to Shah Shuja-al-Mulk. A British attempt to make an alliance with him fell through and he was deposed, fleeing to India. In 1826 Dost Mohammed Khan of the Berakhzai clan made himself ruler of Kabul and Ghazni and took the title of Amir, or King, in 1835, a few years before the British invaded his country.

There were – and possibly to a lesser extent since recent troubles, still are – many ethnic groups resulting from Afghanistan's geographical position as a corridor between India and the countries to the north and west. Tribal loyalties and rivalries in the early nineteenth century were intense. Half the population were Pushtoons, or Pathans, who speak Pushto and there were a great many sub-tribes fiercely loyal to their own group. Although mostly nomadic pastoralists they could easily become aggressive given a pretext. Less warlike than the Pushtoons were the Tadjiks in the north and west who spoke Farsi (Persian), the Uzbegs, the Turkomen and others. The Hazaras from the mountains west of Kabul were the only Shias in a nation of Sunnis and the Kuzzilbash, who lived in and near Kabul, had little in common with the Pushtoon amongst whom there were the sub-tribes of Mahsuds, Wazirs, Yusufzais, Duranis and Ghilzais who figure largely in later chapters. The one great bond between them all was Pushtoon-wallah, the name given to tribal law and ancient custom binding on all of them. These included the law of sanctuary whereby an enemy was safe and entertained hospitably so long as he was under his host's roof; but once he left he became a target. There were also rigid laws of retaliation and of a life for a life, although this could sometimes be commuted to cash payment.

All these people became known to the British just as 'Afghans', about whom certain generalisations were common. An anonymous British officer taking part in the war of 1839-42 wrote, '. . . If the men were more correct in their conduct, virtue would be more common among their women but it is humiliating to be obliged to declare that the men of this country are addicted to the most unnatural and disgusting of vices. The moral character of the Affghan (sic) ranks very low in the scale . . .' He went on to write that no Afghan could be trusted except when a guest was actually under his roof. He described the women walking the streets as being

> covered from head to foot in a white sheet which covers both front and rear like a herald's coat and fits rather close to the head, that part which covers the eyes is of a kind of network which enables the fair lady to see everything that is going on but her features are invisable (sic). They generally walk badly and have nothing of the grace and freedom of Hindustanee women. What their figures and features may be when freed from the most unbecoming dress I cannot say from personal observation but from enquiries I have made they are described as having generally round and chubby broad faces, the eyes and the complexion rather fair. In the streets you see some rather pretty children if the little beasts would only wash their faces and blow their noses. The women are by no means famed for chastity but this is more their misfortune than their fault . . .

Outsiders' views of other people are usually distorted and the legend is preferred to truth. Afghans believe that the British were soundly beaten in all three wars between 1839 and 1919 whereas on two occasions the bulk of the British/Indian forces withdrew, having once captured the capital, leaving the remainder to be defeated before an army of retribution returned. According to Louis Dupree who made many oral records of conversations, they remain convinced that the British are cowards and are untrustworthy (see Bibliography).

A truer view of Afghan society is given in the book written by Morag Murray, a Scots girl who married the son of an Afghan chief less than 100 years after the First Afghan War, in which she quoted her husband as saying,

> We – that is, my clan – look upon our women with the greatest respect. The care we lavish on them and our anxiety to protect them from any harm has gained for us the reputation of making slaves of them. That is not the case. We revere them, and the worst crime in my hills is abduction. I have no wish to claim another man's bride. Such a thing at home would cause clan warfare which would not stop until every male member of the offending one's clan had been wiped out.

Morag went out to make a happy marriage, in which she was fully accepted by her husband's people; and on one occasion joined the other women in keeping up a heavy fire from the fort on intruders who had taken advantage of the men's absence [see Bibliography].

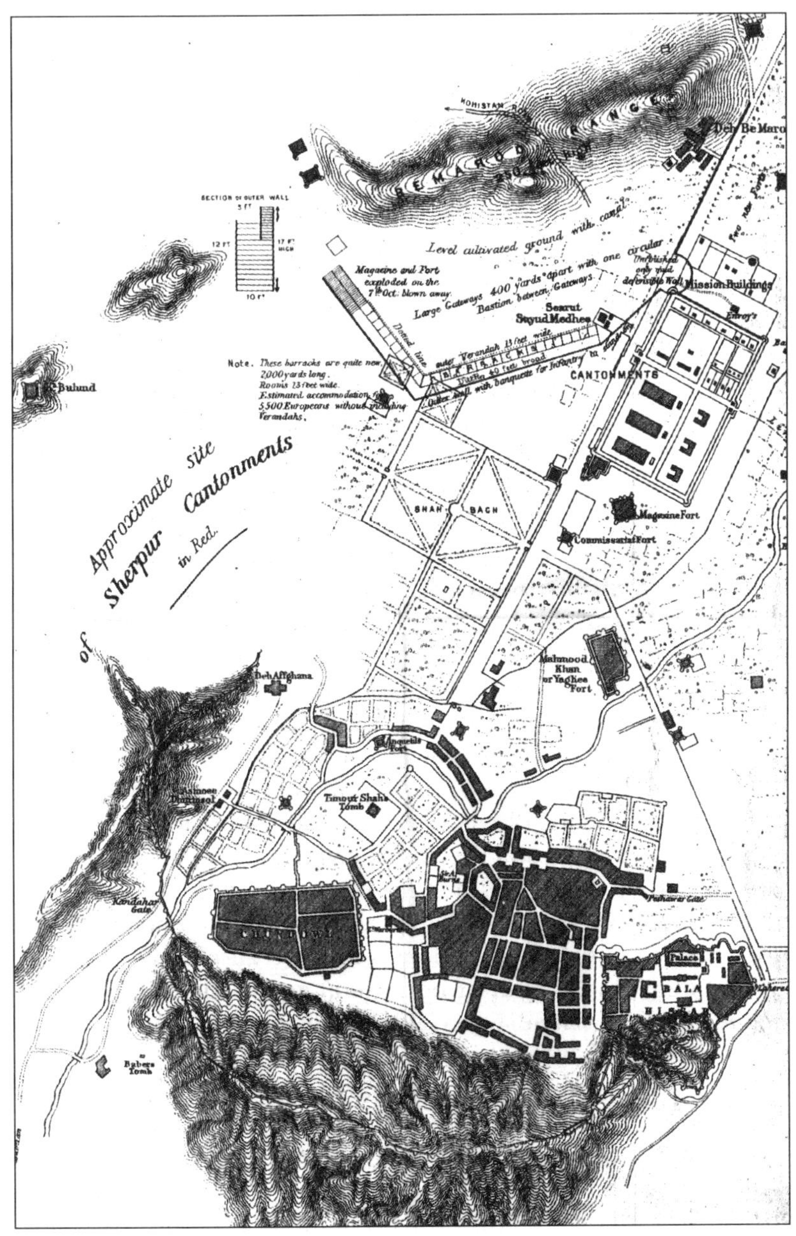

Map A: Kabul and its environs, 1842.

CHAPTER II

A Quick War and a False Peace

British policy towards Afghanistan was dictated by events on the world stage. In the eighteenth century Peter the Great of Russia had despatched an ill-fated expedition to central Asia and later there had been another projected venture between the Tsar and Napoleon to drive towards India, which was aborted by events elsewhere. A number of British officers saw in the southward expansion of Russia a threat to the security of India, such as Moorcroft who in 1825 travelled through Afghanistan, crossing the Oxus which no other European had done, going on to Bokhara where he found that the Russians had been there before him. Yet despite this and other reports from young officers travelling semi-officially beyond India's borders, and despite the Russian annexation of Georgia in 1801 and of 'Russian' Armenia in 1828, no action was taken by successive British governments, of whom the Liberals were always opposed to British expansion and the Tories divided among themselves. It was all bound up also with British relations with Russia on the world stage. The British, alas, became known in central Asia for not adhering to treaty obligations, either because of the changing governments in London or because at a particular time Britain needed Russian friendship in view of events elsewhere. Thus at the beginning of the century, when Persia invoked her treaty with Britain, she was abandoned and instead in 1807 signed a treaty with France. The same happened again when the Russians took Armenia; nor did the British assist the Amirs of Sind, fearful of Afghan expansion. It should be remembered, however, that the British in India were still only servants of a trading company, whose Directors were mainly concerned with profits.

However, by the early 1830s the dangers of Russian expansion southwards towards India were more generally accepted and a number of young officers were supported in their travels, usually in disguise, beyond India's frontiers, to sound out Russian military preparations and opportunities for British commerce. In 1831, Lieutenant Arthur Conolly of the Bengal cavalry failed to reach the Khanate of Khiva although managing to journey from Moscow to India. He saw, better than almost any, that the key lay in Persia and in Herat, then just over the border in Afghanistan. It was in the British interest not to let this key strategic fortified town and its fertile hinterland fall into either Persian or Russian hands.

Lieutenant J.B. Conolly.

Sir Alexander Burnes.

In the same year Lieutenant Alexander Burnes, formerly of the Bombay army, now a political officer, travelled along the Indus river to the court of Ranjit Singh, the famous strong man of the Punjab, the other key strategic area. Officially he took a present of English dray horses, much to the delight of the ruler who had never before seen such huge beasts, whilst also surveying the commercial possibilities of the Indus. He met the deposed Shah Shuja, former ruler of Afghanistan, in Ludhiana and was not impressed, whereas he thought highly of the usurper Dost Mohammed, whose suppression by the British eight years later was to lead to Burnes's death. On this occasion he was hospitably entertained by Dost Mohammed in Kabul before going on to Bokhara. He loved Kabul with its acres of fruit, peaches, plums, apricots and apples and its song birds, nightingales, thrushes and doves; and stayed there on his return journey in 1837, when he found that the Russian Captain Viktevitch was already there. Indeed, young Russian officers were as active as their British counterparts, usually with more support from their government.

In 1837 Lieutenant Eldred Pottinger, who was to be one of the hostages four years later, was also in Afghanistan gathering military intelligence, and when the Persians laid siege to Herat, with the Russian Colonel Simonich conspicuous among the

Major E. Pottinger.

attackers, although officially only an observer, Pottinger gave active assistance to the defence, becoming known in the English press as the 'Hero of Herat'. Others in Afghanistan at that time included Charles Masson, a perceptive observer and traveller, posing as an American but in reality a deserter from the Bengal artillery, and Lieutenant Witkiwicz, a Pole in the Russian service who had delivered letters to Dost Mohammed from the Tsar and the Shah of Persia. These activities, together with Dost Mohammed's request for Britain to oppose Ranjit Singh, whose territories had once been in Afghan hands, frightened the British authorities in India. Lord Auckland, the Governor-General, took the advice of Sir William MacNaghten, then head of the secret and political services of the Government of India, and in 1838 signed treaties with Ranjit Singh and Shah Shuja. Under this, Shuja relinquished claims to Sikh lands and was to be assisted by Ranjit Singh in an attempt to get back his throne. In effect, the wily old one-eyed Ranjit Singh was more interested in securing his Sutlej river boundary against the British, against whom, however, he had no intention of fighting. That was to come after his death some years later.

The plan was for Shah Shuja to lead his own force to Kandahar and for his son, Shahzade Taimur, assisted by a Sikh force, to go from Peshawar to Kabul. Above all, Ranjit Singh did not want the British to take the direct road to Kabul through Lahore and Peshawar. Karnal, near Ambala, became the British advance cantonment with outposts at Ludhiana and Ferozepore. The Shah's force under seconded British officers was raised throughout Bengal and Oudh in 1838, from the same classes as the East India Company's Bengal Native Infantry[1] and Cavalry with the exception of one Gurkha battalion and some Pathans. All were armed with smoothbore muskets.

The Bengal troops of the East India Company's contingent were concentrated at Ferozepore where the Shah's force had assembled by the end of October 1839 when the news came of the raising of the siege of Herat by the Persians, which had the effect of reducing the number of troops for the invasion as the Russians, said to be behind the Persians, were no longer seen as a threat – for the time being. In December the Bengal troops

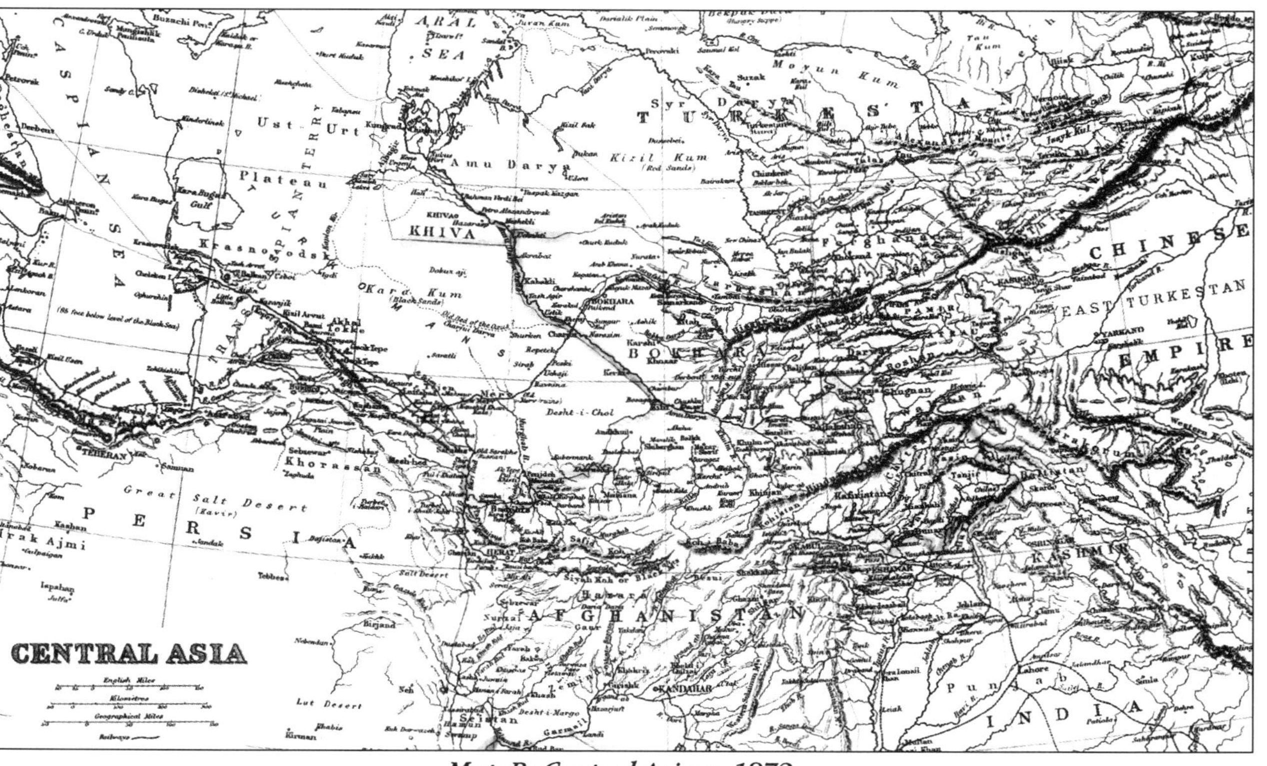

Map B: Central Asia c. 1872.

moved down the left bank of the Sutlej river to Shikarpur, crossing the Indus at Sukhur, following behind the Shah's force. Meanwhile Shahzade Taimur's contingent moved on Peshawar.

The Shah had about 6,000 men; the Bengal troops numbered 9,000 of whom about a third were British, including the officers in 'Native' units; and the Bombay troops in reserve came to 6,000. There was an edict against excess baggage but one Lancer officer had forty servants and one of the generals had forty-three baggage camels, while most officers had a train of servants and grooms. The main force crossed over the Bolan pass to Quetta (now in Pakistan) where the troops concentrated, leaving behind one cavalry and two infantry regiments under General Nott, who were to play a significant role later on. Crossing the Khojah pass they had to make slides to lower the guns to transport carts as it was so steep but they kept going against limited opposition. On 25 April 1839 Shah Shuja made a triumphal entry into Kandahar whose provincial government had left and whose inhabitants made little show of welcome. By the beginning of May the whole force, including the Shah's and the East Indian Company's Bengal troops, but not including Taimur's, were concentrated at Kandahar where they remained for two months to recuperate, having been on half rations for a month and having lost 20 per cent of the cavalry horses, dead from starvation.

At the end of that time, after stores had been replenished and supplies collected locally, General Sir John Keane started moving on Kabul with 8,000 of the Company's troops and 4,000 of the Shah's, leaving a garrison at Kandahar. The main obstacle to their advance was the fortress city of Ghazni which was stormed on 23 August by two columns, including the light companies of HM's 2nd, 13th and 17th of Foot, the Bengal European regiment and the reserve of the 16th, 35th and 48th N.I. under Sir Willoughby Hatton. The guns opened up half an hour before daylight to distract the enemy's attention from the gate where in due course 300 pounds of powder in fifteen bags were ignited. The 9-pounders of the artillery played on it and there was a tremendous explosion. 'Never did I behold a more magnificent sight' wrote an anonymous officer. A storming party managed to get in but were forced back temporarily and at the same time all the enemy guns fired at the British cavalry who had formed a cordon round the fort. The result of all this and of a false rumour of failure caused Brigadier (acting Major General) Sale and his reinforcements to sound the retreat, but they were stopped by the cheers of their comrades now in the fort. They promptly advanced again in time to meet a rush of escaping fugitives. Desperate at finding their route blocked, they threw themselves at the 17th in hand-to-hand fighting in which Sale – of whom much more anon – received a sabre wound in the face and his horse lost its footing. He rolled down the hillside with his opponent who, fortunately for Sale, was killed by Captain Kershaw with a sword thrust. Of the Afghans, the unknown officer wrote: 'Nothing could exceed the desperation with which they defended themselves . . . during the rest of the day we were engaged in the work of slaughter in the town.' British casualties, according to him, were 170 killed and wounded; and 300 enemy bodies were counted, although other estimates put these figures much higher.

Another diarist, Lieutenant Trower, had been with Shah Shuja's force at the storming of Ghazni and had been much impressed by the Sikhs and by one of their French officers, a Colonel Mouton.

On 7 August Shah Shuja and Sir William MacNaghten, the British Envoy, rode through Kabul. The crowd was quietly respectful but certainly not as great as MacNaghten made out to Lord Auckland. MacNaghten was one of the intellectuals of the political department, being proficient in Persian as well as Hindi and other Indian languages. He had begun his career as a soldier but most of his service had been civil: as political assistant at Mysore, joint magistrate, judge and High Court registrar; and he had passed examinations in both Hindu and Mohammedan law. He had become head of the 'Secret and Political' department of the Government of India and Auckland's trusted adviser. He had proposed the deposition of Dost Mohammed and had engineered the tripartite treaty between the Government of India,[2] Ranjit Singh and Shah Shuja. His failings, an incurable optimism merging on wishful thinking and a profound belief in his own diplomatic abilities, were to contribute to disaster,

Sir William MacNaghten.

although his military secretary and political assistant, Captain George Lawrence, ascribed the blame mainly to others. Lawrence was the third son of a famous Indian family. His father, Colonel Lawrence, was well known for his martial exploits in India, his brother John was to end up as Governor-General, while another brother Henry was the mortally wounded hero of the siege of Lucknow seven years later. A fourth brother became a Major General in India.

The Bombay contingent now returned to India, sacking Kalat on the way in order to punish the inhabitants for withholding supplies; and the British in Kabul settled down to enjoy themselves in this new garrison. During 1840 a number of officers' wives arrived, bungalows were built, gardens created, horse racing instituted and a lively social life began in which some of the leading Afghans participated. There was a degree of mutual admiration between British and Afghans for their sporting prowess and horsemanship and all seemed set fair, especially as Dost Mohammed was no longer a threat. He had at first raised a contingent of Uzbeg horsemen and then, coming closer to Kabul, another of Tadjiks from Kohistan and had had some military successes before surrendering to MacNaghten in person. The Envoy was out riding with Lawrence when a horseman caught hold of his bridle crying, according to Lawrence, 'The Ameer, the Ameer,' followed by another horseman who rapidly dismounted, seizing hold of MacNaghten's stirrup leather, and then took his hand which he put to his forehead and lips as a sign of submission. Sir William instantly dismounted and said, 'You are welcome, you are welcome,' and rode back with him to his quarters where the Dost prostrated himself with his forehead on the floor. He then delivered up his sword which MacNaghten returned to him, assuring him of every consideration by the British. Dost Mohammed asked after his family, at that time in British hands at Ghazni, and wrote, through a letter-writer, to tell his sons, who had not been there, to surrender. He said that he had decided to do so despite a recent successful action against Sale's force, and had ridden off with just a few personal followers. A few days later he was sent off under escort to India.

Although there now seemed to be total tranquillity there were rumblings under the surface. In April Ghilzais had attacked a British force at Tezeen, between Kandahar and Ghazni and there had been skirmishes near Bameean, where the Gurkhas[3] had distinguished themselves. So too had the locally recruited Uzbeg Horse – recruited from the same source as Dost Mohammed's followers. There had also been British reverses in Kohistan and the Envoy had been pressing for reinforcements which were never forthcoming. Now, however, with the Dost's surrender, all seemed to be well and British soldiers were able to walk unarmed in the bazaars. The Afghans respected only rulers with

Captain George Lawrence.

power and it became increasingly obvious that although MacNaghten ostensibly had control only over foreign policy he was really the de facto ruler of the country and even the restless Ghilzais, who had been given a substantial subsidy to keep the peace, were passively prepared to accept the situation – for the time being.

However, Shah Shuja enjoyed all the outward trappings of power and relations with the British were cordial, even though there were rumours that he had been doing some double dealing with the Sind Amirs, and a number of leading Afghans attended his court. This was the time of decision for the British,

Shah Shuja.

having succeeded in their object of replacing Dost Mohammed with Shuja. They could either leave, having achieved their objectives, or they could reinforce the army and virtually take over Afghanistan, under whatever political guise, as a buffer against possible Persian and Russian aggression. Although well aware of these options, Auckland took no decision at all. The troops were ordered out of the safety of the Bala Hissar citadel into cantonments built on the plain outside the town and more wives were encouraged to join their husbands.

The winter passed without incident but some of the more prescient of the political officers were already doubtful about the future. George Lawrence, who had been at the attack on Ghazni with his regiment, the 2nd Bengal Light Cavalry, before joining MacNaghten, had had a prophetic meeting before the attack with a well-dressed Afghan horseman who had seen the British in camp and said, 'You are an army of tents and camels; our army is one of men and horses . . . what could induce you to squander scores of rupees in coming to a poor rocky country like ours, without wood or water, and all in order to force upon us a ***kumbukht*** [an unlucky person] as a king, who the moment you turn your backs, will be upset by Dost Mohammed, our own king?' Despite his intense loyalty to MacNaghten, Lawrence had felt from the beginning that the British had been misled by the endemic feuding between the Afghan chiefs on the assumption that they would never coalesce to prevent Shah Shuja from assuming the throne. He wrote of the Afghans, 'possessing many noble qualities . . . there was much calculated to prepossess us in favour of the Afghans as a people on first acquaintance. Further exposure however proved them to be destitute of all regard to truth; treacherous, revengeful and bloodthirsty, sensual and avaricious to a degree not to be comprehended by those who have not lived among them, and thus become intimately acquainted with their character . . .' He wrote these words, however, long after the murder of his chief and his own incarceration but in the beginning he shared the general view of the Afghans' qualities. He may well, however, have shared the view held by a number of officers, including Brigadier Sir Alexander Burnes, the Resident (second in hierarchy to MacNaghten, the Envoy), that the British were backing the wrong horse, comparing unfavourably Shah Shuja's haughty demeanour with Dost Mohammed's charm of manner. Many Afghans shared this view as well as becoming disenchanted with the foreigners who were pushing up prices and taking their women so easily. One of the few apparently to do this legally was Lieutenant Robert Warburton, acting as Captain in charge of the Shah's artillery and later to be one of the hostages. He had taken part in the storming of Ghazni and had settled down in Kabul City, in common with other British officers serving as specialists with the Shah's troops. There, in November 1840, he married Shah Jehan

Begum, daughter of Abdul Raheen Khan, in the presence of Burnes, who had no such scruples about marriage and was well known for the number of his mistresses, of Colonel Jenkins, and of several Afghan witnesses. The marriage contract consisted of six lakhs of rupees, jewellery and furniture. This all seems very praiseworthy until Warburton's later conduct is considered in Chapter V.

The Begum had been married before, to Sirdar Faiz Talab Khan, a high official in Dost Mahommed's service who had divorced her – why we know not. She was a niece of the Dost although also related to Shah Shuja and as such was a noble lady, known as a Princess. There are a number of unexplained circumstances, chief of which is why she ever married Warburton. She was famous for her wealth and beauty and had twin daughters as well as a boy by her first husband. Family tradition on the distaff side has it that Warburton abducted her but this hardly explains the marriage certificate in which she is 'given away' by her father. According to the family version it was during the absence of her husband on an official mission that this took place. Warburton apparently sent her, through a bribed agent, a message to the effect that her husband had sent her an

The Shah's Horse Artillery.

urgent letter by a certain mullah and that as it contained matters of a profoundly secret and important nature she was to go quietly to his house where it would be delivered to her as the mullah had strict instructions not to give it into any hands but hers. Accompanied by her son she went by palanquin to the house where she was shut into a room. The palanquin bearers, who had been bribed, then ran away. She found herself in the presence of a young British officer who pointed a pistol at her and said that it would be useless for her to try and return to her husband and friends who would have assumed that she had joined him of her own free will. He then told her that he had arranged to place her under the protection of her uncle Sirdar Mahommed Khan in whose house she was to be concealed until he could arrange to marry her. In due course her husband divorced her, retaining the two daughters whom she never saw again. There are some faults and anomalies in this version which refers to Warburton as an ensign and states that Lieutenant Eyre – another of the hostages – was present at the ceremony, although he is not mentioned on the marriage certificate as being a witness. Possibly the truth is that there was a degree of coercion. Nevertheless she remained with him until his death, going with him to various Indian cantonments. The strangest thing of all is why Mahommed Akbar Khan should have involved himself, unless he had a score to settle with her husband or father; for he was to become the chief of those who searched for her during the nine months when she was in hiding, going from house to house of relatives and friends, whilst her husband was a hostage in Kabul.

Be all that as it may, there is no doubt that British officers and men, following the example set by Burnes, did play fast and loose with Afghan women; and this was one of the causes of disaffection.

In April 1841 the country appeared to be quiet when Major General Elphinstone took over command at the age of fifty-nine, but already, in Indian terms, an old and sick man who was the worst possible choice, although the British troops liked him. He had served with distinction at Waterloo, and had purchased the Lieutenant Colonelcy of HM's 33rd of Foot two years before,

Lieutenant Vincent Eyre.

after serving as a major in the West Indies Regiment. In 1839 he had taken command of the Benares division.

The following month Major Pottinger, the political agent for Kohistan, told the Envoy that there were insufficient troops there but MacNaghten thought he was being alarmist. Pottinger, who was to play a leading role in the fortunes of the hostages, had travelled in Afghanistan disguised as a horse trader, one of the players of the Great Game, finding out information about the country and likely Russian invasion routes, before becoming the 'Hero of Herat'.

Early in October 1841 three Ghilzai chiefs and their followers took up positions at strong points at the Khoord Kabul defile only ten miles from the city, effectively cutting off communications with India. At the same time intelligence was received that Mahommed Akbar, second son of Dost Mahammed, had arrived at Bameean in order to intrigue against the Government. Although urged by his father to give himself up he had refused to do so; and the mounting hostility in the east was ascribed to his intrigues. The main reason, however, was that the subsidies to the Ghilzais had been stopped by the parsimonious Government in India, always aware of the commercial attitude of the directors of the East India Company.

Meanwhile Major General Sale's brigade left to take up winter quarters in Jelalabad and from thence to return to India (whilst Lady Sale stayed on for the time being in Kabul). On 11 October he left Kabul with HM's 13th of Foot (later the Somerset Light Infantry; now part of the Light Infantry Regiment), the 35th and 37th N.I. and supporting arms. He was fired on at the Khoord Kabul pass, the advance guard ahead of the main body having already lost thirty-five sepoys killed and wounded. The enemy were behind sangars, breast-high defences made of rock or stone, ideal in country where it was impossible to dig, on the high ground above the narrowest part of the gorge, as well as the topmost heights. Sale tried to force the pass despite the heavy and accurate fire directed on his brigade, but halfway through the defile a company of the 13th and another of the 35th N.I. were again fired on. They returned fire and sent flanking parties struggling up the heights with sappers to deal with the sangars. The main body now caught up with them, including Sale who had been wounded in the leg. They pushed on to Khoord and on the 27th Captain MacGregor, the political officer for the area, marched on to Tazean, where, despite enemy opposition, he was joined by Sale. The governor of the Ghilzai area was arrested and put in prison. On the 26th Sale resumed his march, Macgregor having cajoled the Ghilzais to sign a treaty, of which Lieutenant Vincent Eyre wrote, '. . . it proved to be a most hollow truce; for the term "treaty" can scarcely be applied to any agreement made with men so proverbially treacherous as the whole race of Afghans have proved themselves to be . . .' (Both Lawrence and

Eyre wrote after their nine months captivity which affected their outlook. In our day those same Afghans would be called 'freedom fighters' opposing an unjustified invasion and replacement of a good king by a bad one.)

Despite the seriousness of the Ghilzais uprising the British in Kabul felt so secure that the property of Elphinstone, who was relinquishing his command because of ill health, and MacNaghten, who was due to become Governor of Bombay, fetched high prices at auction. In the event, neither of them was destined ever to leave Afghanistan alive. Lawrence did not share the general complacency and wrote, 'Ever since our entrance into the country, the population of Afghanistan, with one or two short intervals, had been in a state of rebellion against the Shah's authority. To live in a state of insurrection and turmoil is indeed congenial to the tastes and habits of the people and our presence rather encouraged than kept under natural propensities.' He thought that Shah Shuja might possibly have succeeded on his own without the irritant of the British presence (not unlike the situation after the Russian withdrawal in the 1980s) but that Dost Mohammed was stronger than Shah Shuja. He was 'an energetic, determined character, fearing neither God nor man and holding all pledges even of the most solemn descriptions mere moonshine when they stood in his way, rendered him a very fit person to rule and keep in subordination, through dread of his authority, this turbulent and implacable people'. In the end, however, he proved to be a wise ruler and a good ally.

On 2 November a messenger sent by Lawrence into the city to make a few purchases, returned breathless, in the greatest state of excitement saying that the shops were all closed and that crowds of armed men filled the streets, surrounding the houses of Burnes and Captain Johnson, the paymaster, which had been set on fire. Lawrence went with MacNaghten to a meeting with Elphinstone and senior officers, at which Captain Mackenzie produced a note from Burnes begging for aid as the tumult was increasing and he feared that his house was going to be attacked. To start with, it had been no more than an outbreak by a few disaffected chiefs and their followers which rapid military action would have quelled. It began with an attack by a mere 300 men on the compound of Burnes's house and that of Captain Johnson who held the funds[4] for the British forces. At first Burnes, who had infinite faith in his own political abilities to deal with Afghans, forbad his guard to fire and harangued the mob from a gallery of his house. This achieved nothing and when the place was stormed by the inflamed mob, they had to fight for it. Burnes, his young brother, Lieutenant Burnes, Broadfoot of the Bengal European regiment and every man, woman and child on the premises were killed. Yet only the night before Burnes had been warned of the danger, which he had shrugged off. Vincent Eyre voiced the feelings of many of the junior officers when he wrote, 'No man, surely, in a highly responsible public situation – especially in such a one as the late Sir Alexander Burnes – ought ever to indulge in a state of blind security or to neglect salutary warnings, however small . . .'

Back at the cantonment, Lawrence proposed that a battalion be sent to reinforce Burnes, not then knowing that the worst had happened, and that detachments should be sent to arrest known ringleaders such as Amenullah Khan and Abdullah Khan but this was 'at once set down as one of pure insanity and under the circumstances, utterly unfeasible'. A suggestion that Brigadier Shelton's force should be sent to the Bala Hissar was accepted, but not for an immediate move, merely for the troops to get ready. The message was taken by Lieutenant Sturt, Lady Sale's son-in-law, an engineer officer who had been critical of the defences of the cantonment.

Meanwhile, Shah Shuja, unaware of Burnes's murder and the stealing of £17,000 from Johnson's house, but realizing that something was afoot, sent his son to the city with his retainers and Campbell's regiment of sepoys from his own force, but the reinforcements that could have crushed the insurrection never arrived. Shelton had at last received orders to leave his position, one and a half miles from the cantonment, and march to the Bala Hissar, so had set off with one company of HM's 44th Regiment of Foot (later the Essex Regiment and now part of the Royal Anglians), a wing of the 54th N.I., five 6-pounder field guns, the 6th Regiment of the Shah's infantry and four horse artillery guns.

He was ordered to use his own judgement as to the action to be taken, having consulted Shah Shuja, and to send the rest of his brigade back to the cantonment. These consisted of the remainder of the 44th, two horse artillery guns and Anderson's Irregular Horse. At the same time a message was sent to the 37th N.I. to recall them from Khoord Kabul. With hindsight, and in the light of what followed, both the orders were inept. An earlier order had been sent to Sale to return to Kabul and this would, if carried out, have strengthened the garrison just before the uprising, but Sale, with the support of his officers, decided to ignore it and continue southwards towards Gandamuk on the grounds that most of his ammunition had been expended and that they could never have repassed the Ghilzais' positions with all his wounded. His personal preference would no doubt have been to rejoin his wife and daughter in Kabul but had he obeyed Elphinstone's order his remnants would hardly have raised morale in the cantonment. In the event, the presence of a garrison at Jelalabad prepared to make sorties and be a thorn in the Afghans' flesh, turned out to be beneficial to the British.

Lawrence was sent off to cover the two miles direct to the Bala Hissar to report the situation, taking with him the four troops of the Envoy's escort. Mounted on a powerful horse belonging to Sir William, he ordered his men to keep going under all circumstances and on no account to stop. They encountered an Afghan who rose out of a ditch lunging with a huge sword at Lawrence who threw a stick at him before the escort shot him with their carbines. Their rapid pace got them through the troubled countryside, reaching their objective without casualties. Had Elphinstone acted swiftly and sent larger forces at the same high speed to the Bala Hissar and to the city they would almost certainly have been successful. Lawrence found the Shah walking up and down in great agitation in the court before the throne. 'Is it not what I always told the Envoy would happen if he would not follow my advice?' he exclaimed. He was referring to his request to MacNaghten that certain chiefs should be seized and executed; which MacNaghten had refused to do.

Lawrence asked the Shah to authorize Shelton to advance and occupy the Bala Hissar but the King replied that it would be

The Bala Hissar.

better to wait for news from his son, Futtijung, and Prime Minister Mahommed Osman Khan who had advanced into the city with some of the Shah's troops with apparently some success. Meanwhile a number of British officers in the city were having their own problems. Captain Trevor, paymaster to the Shah's troops, lived with his wife and seven children in a defendable tower by the riverside, with a sepoy guard, near the quarter of the city inhabited by Kuzzilbash, who had no great love for Pushtoons. It was opposite the fort occupied by Brigadier Anquetil and the Shah's contingent, close to the house occupied by Captain Troup, Brigade Major to the Shah's force. He and Anquetil had ridden out early in the morning and were now cut off and unable to get back. Captain MacKenzie's house was also under siege at the same time.

Whilst Lawrence was still with the Shah, Lieutenant Sturt rushed in, sword in hand, bleeding profusely. As he was dismounting at the gate of the Bala Hissar he had been attacked and stabbed three times in the face and throat by a man who

Captain Colin Mackenzie.

rushed out of the crowd round the entrance and then made his escape. Lawrence washed and staunched Sturt's wounds before sending him back to the camp in one of the Shah's palanquins.

The Shah's advisers were now recommending the recall of Futtijung and the Prime Minister but Lawrence thought they should stay in the city whilst regretting that there were no British troops with them. Nevertheless the Shah did order their withdrawal. Before long Mahommed Osman Khan entered: 'a bold, honest, uncompromising man . . . panting from the fray and, greatly excited, said in an angry tone to the King, "By recalling us just at the moment of victory your troops will be

Prince Futtijung.

defeated and evil will fall on all."' Lawrence successfully entreated to the Shah to send him to Shelton whom he reached in the Seah Shah cantonment between the main British force and the Bala Hissar; Shelton acted swiftly, setting out himself with a squadron of the 5th Light Cavalry, a company of HM's 4th of Foot, a wing of the 54th N.I., four horse artillery guns and the Shah's 6th infantry.

Lawrence then returned to his post at the side of the Envoy who was delighted to see him as his death had been reported, and only reluctantly let him return to Shelton who asked for his services as interpreter. Before doing so he tried to give what comfort he could to Lady Sale about the condition of Sturt, her son-in-law. He then rode off with Captains Troup and Johnson with a strong escort to the Bala Hissar where they found the Shah still walking about the court with his officers. Shelton was directing fire on the city with two of his guns and the enemy were returning fire with jezzails.[5] Captain Macintosh, the Brigade Major, was shot through his forage cap as they talked. Lawrence told the others that Shelton's conduct amazed him 'beyond expression'. Later he wrote, 'I confess to a doubt having crossed my mind before then, as to whether, if tried, he would not be found a failure but I as often dismissed it as unjust to the man . . . he was dissatisfied with his position, a great croaker and anxious to return to India. Such was the man who, alas, was destined to exercise so baneful an influence over our fortunes at this period of unexplained peril . . . with incapacity stamped on every feature of his face.' He had announced that his force was inadequate to enter the city at once but was prepared to place the two guns on an elevated place in the Bala Hissar in order to fire down the street into the city, but that was all.

The Shah was understandingly angry at the lack of any substantial British support; and although Shelton had been made

Captain C. Troup.

aware of this, he was, in Lawrence's words, 'quite paralysed'. In the evening of this dreadful long day of 2 November, Lawrence considered that his presence at the Bala Hissar was of little value, as the Brigadier ignored his suggestions and the Shah's bodyguard had been recalled at the very moment of apparent victory in the city. Both the Bala Hissar and the cantonment force now appeared to be isolated. Lawrence returned to the cantonment with Troup and Johnson, both of whom had been spared by the mob who had claimed only to want vengeance on Burnes.

CHAPTER III

An Avoidable Disaster

On his return, Lawrence found that Sir William had left the Residency in Kabul and with Lady MacNaghten had moved into the cantonment. By now he had heard of Burnes's death, the plundering of Johnson's treasury and that Trevor and Mackenzie were still holding out with a handful of men. As both had sent urgent requests for assistance Lawrence suggested sending in two companies of infantry to help with them but this was condemned by the staff as 'imprudent'.

> What a contrast [he wrote] to the vacillation of our military commanders did the conduct of these two gallant officers exhibit, proving by their successful resistance, although wounded, the weakness at that time of the mob, and how easily we could have quelled the insurrection had we only... used the powerful force at our disposal, but alas, vacillation and incapacity ruled in our military councils. Of those in authority the Envoy alone comprehended the gravity of the crisis and showed his usual resolution and strength of character...

Unfortunately, MacNaghten, although the senior British official, was a civilian, despite his early military background, and had no power to do more than urge his views for immediate action on the military commanders. He was, however, the originator of the orders given by Elphinstone for Sale to return by forced marches from Gandamuk to Kabul, which, in the event proved impossible; and for Nott's brigade not to return to India. They too were unable to get to Kabul but proved their worth by garrisoning Kandahar. 'The energy and decision which characterised the chief civil authority were alas altogether wanting in our military leaders,' wrote Lawrence, who described General Elphinstone as being:

> so prostrated in mind and body by a severe and protracted suffering from fever and rheumatic gout, that he was perfectly incapable of exertion . . . enfeebled as he was in body and mind by disease General Elphinstone was completely in the hands of his staff and although there were several noble exceptions among them, as a body they were characterised by the most deplorable vacillation and absence of energy. . . thus the 2nd November slowly waned away and at last closed in apathy and confusion . . .

Captain Colin Mackenzie had been sent to Kabul to recuperate from fever and the heat in Peshawar, and was in Kohistan when the insurrection started. He volunteered to go with Sale's brigade to clear the Khoord and Kabul passes and had joined Broadfoot's newly raised corps of sappers and miners. He was in the thick of the fighting at the breastworks up on the hill above the narrowest part of the gorge. Later he took charge of Shah Shuja's commissariat at the fort of Nishan Khan a mile and a half from the cantonment. On the morning of the 2nd he heard of the riot in the city but not of Burnes's murder. 'Suddenly', he was to write later, 'a naked man stood before me, covered with blood from two deep sabre cuts in the head and five musket shots in the arm and body.' He was a messenger from MacNaghten who had failed to reach Trevor. After this, Mackenzie closed the gates of his compound and made his men stand to arms. Back in the cantonment when this was reported, Lawrence volunteered to go to Mackenzie's aid but was refused by Elphinstone himself. At midday on the 3rd Mackenzie saw the enemy swarming into Trevor's house but fortunately Trevor and his wife and family had managed to slip away on foot.

Mackenzie continued to hold out for another forty-eight hours with his ninety loyal Afghan Jezzailchees, twenty sepoys and some sappers until their ammunition ran out. Although wounded, he had even been able to make several counter-attacks. Of his performance, Lawrence wrote, 'What a comment was his spirited defence on the supineness of our commanders.' Although without ammunition, he and his men had made a rush for the cantonment, Mackenzie severing the arm of his assailant before being knocked from the saddle by a blow on the back of his head. Fortunately one of his men came to his aid and got him

The Khoord Kabul Pass.

to safety. Later some friendly Afghan chiefs told him that if only he had been reinforced by a couple of battalions, the British could have retaken the city. Major Broadfoot, who commanded the sappers, commented that as Mackenzie had been able to cut his way to the cantonment, a much larger force could have cut their way from the cantonment through to him. Instead of any such vigorous action, both the detachment under Shelton near the Bala Hissar and the main body at the cantonment were now under continuous siege.

Whilst some of the British were at or near the Bala Hissar and others were hiding out in the city, the bulk of the force was now confined to the cantonment, whose site had been selected by Burnes together with some army officers, none of whom were engineers or fortification experts, during a period when MacNaghten had been away in Jelalabad. On his return he had expressed his disapproval of a site where the commissariat stores were located outside the entrenchments. He had asked the G.O.I. if he could purchase a number of nearby forts overlooking the cantonment but Auckland had refused permission. So there they were in this low-lying, almost indefensible position instead of in the city and the Bala Hissar.

Fortunately the morale of the force, which had begun to sink, was boosted when Major Griffiths – one of the few heroes of the whole sorry affair – marched in at the head of 37th N.I., two mountain train guns and some of Broadfoot's sappers, having fought their way from the Khoord Kabul pass, as ordered, entering the cantonment in perfect order. 'The arrival of this brave new body of men,' wrote Lawrence, 'greatly cheered the spirits of our troops but did not seem to give much encouragement to our military chiefs or arouse them to greater energy.' However, Shelton, reinforced by a 9-pounder gun, a howitzer and two mortars, was at least keeping up a steady fire on the city, although Lawrence considered that the failure to establish a line of communication to the Bala Hissar through the Lahore gate of the city was due to Shelton's 'negligence'.

The next day Trevor and his family arrived at the cantonment, having been assisted by locally recruited Afghans, some of whom had carried his children on horseback. He told the British commanders that the 15,000 Kuzzilbash and even Dost Mohammed's own clan, the Baruchzyes, had not joined the uprising and if only the British had put on a show of strength they would have been won over. 'Thus,' wrote Lawrence, 'was this second precious day frittered away in endless discussions and abortive proposals instead of in vigorous, instantaneous action.' To make matters worse the garrison even failed to secure the two forts located between the cantonment and the commissariat stores. Vincent Eyre wrote, 'The spoliation of public and private property were perpetuated with impunity within a mile of our cantonment and under the very walls of the Bala Hissar.'

The enemy, normally disunited in true Afghan fashion, were now joining together as they watched with disbelief the inaction in the cantonment, the sluggish movements of Shelton and the discomfiture of the officers in the city. Elphinstone was ill and unable to act decisively and was on the point of recall at his own request. He was highly regarded in the British service but was without much Indian experience and lacked confidence in his own judgement. He was not helped by his subordinates or by MacNaghten who made light of the insurrection, deluding both himself and the General in council. 'The unwelcome truth was soon forced upon us,' wrote Eyre, 'that in the whole Afghan nation, we cannot reckon a single friend.' This however, was patently not true, to judge from the number of friendly acts and warnings experienced by individual British officers. Certainly the Kuzzilbash remained friendly throughout . . .

Some effort was now at last being made to do something about the defences of the cantonment. Eyre, formerly of the Bengal Artillery, who had originally been Commissar of Ordnance for the army volunteered to take charge of the siting of the guns. There were six 9-pounders, three 24-pounder howitzers, one 12-pounder howitzer and three 5½-inch mortars, but Eyre considered that the artillerymen 'fell very short of what was required to man all these effectively, consisting of only 80 Punjabees (sic) belonging to the Shah under Lieutenant Warburton, very insufficiently instructed and of doubtful fidelity.[7] This was a little hard on Warburton for Punjabis had not yet been enlisted in the Company's armies and he had had to take what he could get. Besides, he and his men had done well enough in the attack on Ghazni and with one of the punitive expeditions to the north of Kabul. At that time he was still searching for his wife who was somewhere in the city being hunted by Akbar's vengeful men.

According to Eyre, the cantonment suffered 'from the spirit of false economy which characterised our Afghan policy'. He was amazed that anyone in a half-conquered country should establish troops 'in so extraordinary and injudicious a military position . . . every engineer officer who had been consulted had pointed to the Bala Hissar as the only suitable place . . . the only proper site for the magazine on which the army's efficiency depended . . .' Instead, the cantonment was sited on low swampy ground covered on all sides by hills and forts. A low rampart and a narrow ditch in the form of a parallelogram 1,000 yards by 600 surrounded it, with flanking bastions at each corner. The road ran alongside the Kabul river and a canal; and at the far end of this area was the mission compound, half of which was occupied by MacNaghten and his staff, the rest of the buildings being used for members of the mission and the Envoy's bodyguard, which, in Eyre's opinion, 'rendered the whole face of the cantonment to which it was annexed, nugatory for purposes of defence . . .' To give him credit, Elphinstone had protested as soon as he arrived to take command and had even offered to purchase out of his own pocket a more suitable site; but this had been turned down by the Government in India.

The worst mistake of all was to have the commissariat stores, under Captain Skinner, separated from the main cantonment in an old fort a few hundred yards from the south-west bastion, covered by another fort on the opposite side of the road. In fact, everywhere there were forts commanding fields of fire on to the British below them. They were hemmed in on all sides, so that, in Eyre's words,

> when the rebellion became general the troops could not move out a dozen paces from either gate without their being exposed to the fire from some neighbouring hostile fort, garrisoned too by marksmen who seldom missed their aim . . . almost all the calamities that befell our ill-starred force may be traced more or less to the defects of our position; and our cantonment at Kabul, whether we look to its situation or its construction, must ever be spoken of as a disgrace to our military skill and judgement.

On 5 November the enemy approached the Mohammed Sharrif fort and the Shah Bagh, the Shah's walled garden, only 400 yards from the south-west bastion. They were said to be mining the fort, where the commissariat was defended by only eighty sepoys, and several companies were sent to relieve them. These were repulsed with the loss of two officers killed. Next, the cavalry made a diversion under cover of which the garrison was to withdraw, but this also failed as it was not good country for cavalry, being wooded and intersected by watercourses. Twenty-two men were killed in this abortive affair.

Worried that there were only two days' worth of supplies within the cantonment, MacNaghten pressed the General to secure the commissariat fort, but only after three hours of discussion was it finally agreed that there should be an assault. By the time this was finally agreed it was too late, for Lieutenant Warren and his eighty men of the commissariat guard had been forced to withdraw. 'Shortly after,' wrote Lawrence, 'the enemy could be seen in swarms removing all our stores, the daily bread of our troops, and apparently careless about any ill-conceived and futile demonstration we could make to prevent them.'

On the 6th a successful assault was launched against the Mohammed Sharrif fort by the indomitable Major Griffiths with three companies of HM's 44th of Foot and elements of the 5th and 7th regiments N.I. Although a young ensign was shot through the heart whilst waving the colours on one of the walls, the attack was a success, a cavalry charge finally dispersing the enemy who were pursued right into the city, many being sabred in the streets. At the same time Mackenzie and his Afghans drove the enemy from the Shah Bagh but were forced to retire when no reinforcements arrived.

The troops were now on half rations but these were supplemented by supplies from the village of Bemarroo, arranged in advance by MacNaghten. Soon, however, these only dribbled in occasionally as the chiefs of the village had now joined the insurgents. The fort and village commanded the rear defences of the camp and although the Envoy, supported by Lawrence, repeatedly pressed for their occupation, together with another fort equally well sited, it was to no avail. Lawrence wrote, 'The gloom and despondency now becoming apparent in our private soldiers who are quick to discern all signs of weakness and incompetency in their leaders, were sufficient to awake the most serious apprehensions, tending as they did to destroy all confidence and spirit of enterprise in our men.'

The Envoy, 'seeing that it was useless to expect any energetic action on the part of the General', urged the recall of Shelton to take over command, 'as poor Elphinstone was quite incapacitated by now'. This was done but Shelton proved to be just as broken a reed, without the mitigation of illness. On the 10th, whilst Lawrence was out riding with the Envoy early in the morning, they saw crowds of enemy horse and foot in the Sung hills preparing to seize the Rikhab Bashee fort, to cut off all British communication with their rear. The General refused to send reinforcements although MacNaghten said he would assume responsibility himself for the outcome. Eventually Shelton agreed but the preparations were so slow that it was not till after three in the afternoon that, led by Shelton himself, a force set out.

The troops consisted of HM's 44th Regiment of Foot, the 37th N.I. and the 6th Shah's infantry with two horse artillery guns. Unfortunately the Afghans had had all day to pour men into the fort which was heavily manned. By mistake the British force only blew up a wicket instead of the main gate so that the attackers could only enter in single file. Even so, they were successful in driving out the enemy until others of the British force still outside yelled that the Afghan cavalry were about to attack. At that, the whole column fled panic-stricken, fired on by the Afghans who had left the fort and were now rallying. An officer who had volunteered to blow in the main gate with a bag of powder was told that neither British nor Indian troops would fight but nevertheless Lawrence saw that Shelton was rallying the men, some of whom had thrown away their arms in flight, and once again he led them into the attack and carried the position. For once Lawrence was generous in Shelton's praise and for the 'gallant and energetic manner in which he recalled his troops and led them to retake the fort'. Not only that but another three forts were almost destroyed and a good supply of grain was brought into the cantonments. 'These operations', wrote Lawrence, 'although achieved by heavy loss to ourselves – no less than 200 soldiers, chiefly European, having fallen – so completely overawed the enemy that for three days following not an Afghan was to be seen.' Lawrence walked out of the cantonment, covering about three miles, without seeing anyone; and the commissariat camels were able to go out and bring back stores and forage. Had this success been followed up, the city could have been taken. Unfortunately, in Lawrence's words, 'the supineness' of the military chiefs 'meant that partial successes tended rather to weaken than improve their prospects.'

On 13 November, encouraged by the British inactivity, the enemy collected in large numbers on the Bemaroo hills and started to open fire on the cantonment. Once again the Envoy managed to overrule the objections of the military hierarchy and, in Lawrence's words, 'A few men . . . were tardily prepared for the duty under Shelton's command. They took so long about it that MacNaghten had to speak to Shelton in a most peremptory manner.' Even so it was not till 5 o'clock that the troops, consisting of cavalry, infantry, the mountain train and one horse artillery gun, in double column of divisions, advanced towards a gorge in the centre of the range of hills, the cavalry on the right, infantry on the left. They gained the heights and the enemy fled. Once again the troops could have followed them into the city had not night fallen by then. Lawrence wrote,

> Brigadier Shelton thus gained a brilliant success against his own will, but his previous procrastination had rendered it impossible to reap any real advantage from the victory. . . the success of this operation could not fail to inspire our soldiers with contempt of the enemy, showing that Afghans never would withstand a steady and determined advance of our troops. Would that it had produced the salutary effect of inspiring more vigour into our military councils, but in this, alas! it failed.

On the 15th Major Pottinger and Captain Houghton arrived at Lawrence's quarters They had been at Cherekar in Kohistan, where Pottinger was the political agent and Houghton the Adjutant of the Gurkha battalion, to which no reinforcements had been sent. Pottinger and his assistant, Rattray, had been attacked by the leading chiefs of the district who had ostensibly come to negotiate. They managed to withdraw the two miles from the Residency to the garrison at Cherekar fort and after three days' fighting during which the Gurkhas' CO and an ensign were killed, the remaining 200 soldiers withdrew from the fort, together with Pottinger, Rose, Houghton and Dr Grant. Only Pottinger, Houghton and one soldier managed to reach the

British lines. All the others were killed on the way. There was more bad news when it was learnt that Captain Woodburn and 150 men of the Shah's infantry at Shekabad had been massacred 130 miles from Ghazni. They had been inveigled into the courtyard of a fort with the offer of hospitality. The gate then closed and they were fired on from the tower.

General Elphinstone, who had resumed command, now pressed the Envoy to open negotiations. MacNaghten knew that negotiations could only be successful with Afghans from a position of strength but reluctantly agreed to do so because of the recent British successes. He thought that there was a chance of encouraging dissension among the chiefs. At the same time he urged that ammunition should be sent to the Shah at the Bala Hissar and that his earlier proposal of an attack on Mohammed Khan's fort should be accepted. So it was for a time, and then countermanded.

A few days later the Envoy urged that the force should hold out to the last rather than take part in the dishonourable retreat then being considered. This would entail abandoning the Shah, for whom they had entered Afghanistan in the first place, quite apart from there being no shelter for troops in retreat.

On the 22nd the enemy were massed in strength at Bemaroo but a force sent out to clear them away only succeeded in doing some skirmishing in a nearby orchard. Lieutenant Eyre was wounded, shot in the head, but recovered later to be one of the hostages. The next day another attempt was made, under Shelton, to dislodge the Afghans. Fire was opened on them as a large number were seen leaving the village square. Captain Bellew pressed Shelton to follow this up with an assault but the order was not given until the next day, by which time the enemy had returned. They advanced with drums beating and whilst a small party of British was left to watch the village Shelton and the main body took position in close column on the brow of a hill overlooking a gorge beyond which was a hill from where a heavy fire of jezzails was coming, doing great execution on the massed ranks of the British and Indian troops. The leading chief was killed by a shot from Shelton's single gun and panic set in but once again no advantage was taken of this rout of the enemy. The

British stood fast whilst the enemy, who had regrouped, crept up and captured the gun. The troops were ordered to charge in order to retake it but not a man moved so several officers moved to the front to lead a charge, but still no soldier followed them. Two were killed whilst trying to rally the men, and a single brave sepoy engaged in hand-to-hand combat with an Afghan, both falling dead together. 'At last' wrote Lawrence, who was watching from the cantonment, 'the gallant bearing of their officers prevailed with the men, who, advancing, retook the gun, as the enemy fell back.' Once again, the Brigadier was urged to seize the decisive moment to charge but 'nothing could induce him to stir from the field.' Fresh horses, ammunition and limbers were sent for the gun which now reopened fire but when the enemy attacked again the British force broke up in disarray. Lawrence wrote, 'Our squares broke, all order was at an end' and the infantry and cavalry fled downhill and although 'the staunch artillery-men', sword in hand, did their best to save the gun they were forced abandon it. 'I could see from my post,' wrote Lawrence, 'our flying troops hotly pursued and mixed up with the enemy who were slaughtering them on all sides . . .' The survivors poured into the cantonment but were not followed by the pursuing Afghan horsemen who swept to the right of the camp, directed by Mohammed Osman Khan Barukzye, one of the chiefs with whom MacNaghten had been in communication. Fresh troops of the 5th cavalry formed up outside the cantonment, 'under cover of whom some of our flying horsemen rallied, but though the poor decrepit General placed himself at their head, he could not induce them to charge'.

The next day the British, going over the field of battle, discovered that most of the bodies had been mutilated. Lawrence thought that although nothing could justify the conduct of the troops, Shelton was most to blame for the troops had lost all confidence in a leader 'who had proved himself so incapable of command'.

The Afghans were now in a position of strength and therefore willing to negotiate. Some of the chiefs were met by Trevor and Lawrence who had been wounded when acting as ADC to Shelton. Both of them, like Pottinger, Mackenzie, Conolly,

Skinner and other political officers, were Persian speakers, though only Pottinger was fluent also in Pushtu. After long and fruitless discussions they returned to the Envoy with the Afghan demands which were 'speedily and indignantly dismissed . . . being of the most preposterous and inflated character'. This same day, 25 November, General Elphinstone chose to say that he could not hold out without reinforcements and as these were not likely to be forthcoming he recommended opening negotiations with Mohammed Osman Khan who had deflected the Afghan cavalry the previous day.

Afghans in large numbers were seen the following day on the Bemaroo hills whilst all hostilities had been suspended during negotiations. 'As yet,' wrote Lawrence, 'we had not suffered from want of provisions and our single defeat should, instead of daunting have rather stimulated and moved us to energetic action. To strike now a decisive blow, would not only retrieve our own honour, but also, by bringing down the enemy's confidence, induce them to offer us better terms than before.'

These were certainly not forthcoming the next day when the Afghan proposals included abandoning Shah Shuja and unconditional surrender by the British whose lives, however, would be spared. The Envoy broke up the meeting, saying, 'I prefer death to dishonour and leave the issue to the God of battles.'

In the first few days of December nothing much happened except that the enemy failed in an attempt to capture a tower on a hill above the Bala Hissar. Within the cantonment morale was low and discipline had become lax. Major Thain, the Assistant Quartermaster General repeatedly pointed this out to his superiors but as no action followed he took it upon himself to publish an 'Order of the day' about it and to take measures to increase the alertness of the guards.

On 5 December the deceptive calm was broken when the enemy destroyed a bridge over the Kabul river near the cantonment and carried away the timbers before the eyes of the garrison who did nothing about it; and the next day they got Mohammed Sherreef's fort, whose defenders, consisting of a company of HM's 44th of Foot and another of the 37th N.I. fled without firing a shot. When he saw this happening the Envoy hastened to the General's quarters and demanded an immediate attack. This was agreed but put off until nightfall. Lawrence was despatched to find Elphinstone and repeat the instruction to the General, whom he found at one of the bastions with Shelton, still discussing and doing nothing. Sturt and his sappers had set off to reconnoitre a route and Lawrence volunteered to follow him. This was at first agreed and then cancelled – the fate of almost all proposals for action. That day he learnt the shameful news that sentries of the 36th N.I. had been posted to stop men of HM's 44th of Foot from leaving the cantonment on one pretext or another. Yet it was men of this regiment who were to make a heroic last stand at Gandamuk. As always, it all depended on the officers concerned. MacNaghten's proposal to withdraw the 44th from the bazaar area of the cantonment was acted on.

On 8 December the General sent an official letter to the Envoy, the contents of which had been agreed by Brigadiers Shelton and Anquetil and Colonel Charters, stating that no further military operations could be undertaken by the troops in their present condition and that no time should be lost in negotiating a safe return to India. They were prepared to break with the Shah, even though he had kept faith with the British.

MacNaghten, who still hoped for the arrival of reinforcements from Kandahar, told Lawrence to propose to the General that instead of retreat the army should capture the Khowjah Ruwash fort four miles away as it was known to contain large supplies of grain. After much fruitless argument Lawrence had to call the Envoy to attend the meeting in person and ultimately it was agreed. A detachment of the Shah's infantry was prepared and Mackenzie volunteered to take command of the single gun that could be spared. The officer in charge of the cantonment's Kohistan gate was ordered to have the drawbridge down before 4 a.m. with grass spread on the bridge to deaden the noise; but when Mackenzie got there nothing had been done and the officer said he had received no such orders. He ran to tell the Adjutant General, who immediately went to Shelton for orders. Shelton's reaction was merely to inform MacNaghten that the attempt had been abandoned. 'Another instance of the contumacious spirit', wrote Lawrence 'in which all the suggestions of Sir William MacNaghten were set aside, which, if carried out, would have saved the force . . . the military authorities' sole object was to retreat to Hindustan.'

Captain Conolly, with 'our trusty ally Jan Fishan Khan', came to the cantonment to urge the destruction of all stores that could not be moved, the abandonment of the cantonment and occupation of the Bala Hissar, a course already proposed by MacNaghten and Lawrence. Although the General seemed to agree, the plan was opposed by Shelton and MacNaghten said, 'If the General has determined to retreat I cannot of course prevent him; but in that event I will throw myself into the Bala Hissar with the Shah's troops and stand or fall with the King.'

In the event, it was now too late to do anything like that, especially as news was received that the relieving force from Kandahar had failed to get through because of heavy snowfalls. Lawrence remained convinced that any really determined troops could have forced their way through such an early fall.

It was now that the proposal was received from the chiefs for the reopening of negotiations that MacNaghten determined to meet them himself as the military leaders were so supine although his wife begged him not to take any unnecessary risk. The next day he went with Trevor, Mackenzie and Lawrence to a spot 200 yards beyond the ramparts by the Kabul river where most of the chiefs were assembled, including Mohammed Akbar Khan. After an exchange of compliments they all sat on horse cloths spread on the ground and the Envoy produced the draft of an eighteen-article treaty that he had prepared. The main provisions were to the effect that British troops were to return to Peshawar unmolested and given all possible help on their journey, followed by the Ghazni and Kandahar garrisons. The property of officers was to be forwarded to India and at the same time Dost Mohammed's property was to be restored. Shah Shuja was either to remain in Afghanistan with suitable maintenance or allowed to return to India and Dost Mohammed was to resume his throne. The seeds of the hostage concept were sown in the next few words of MacNaghten's proposals, at least on the British side, although the Afghans, who already held some British officers in Kabul, had almost certainly considered it already. 'For the due fulfilment of the above conditions four respectable British officers will be left in Kabul as hostages and will be allowed to return to India on the arrival of the Ameer and his family.' Mohammed Akbar Khan and other chiefs were to accompany the British forces to Peshawar. The Afghans were not to ally themselves with any other power without British assent; a British Resident was to return to Afghanistan if the chiefs wanted it and any Afghans who wanted to return to India with the troops should be allowed to do so. Supplies of stores were to be allowed into the cantonment and any British officers and men unable to return with the army were to be treated with honour and allowed to leave when ready to do so. Apart from the very fact of withdrawal and the return of Dost Mohammed, these were hardly the proposals expected from a military force held in a vice in an indefensible position on half rations. No doubt MacNaghten only put them forward knowing that some would have to be discarded and that, as with all oriental bargaining, the only answer was to make the highest possible bid to start with.

Mohammed Akbar Khan's initial reaction was to treat the proposals with understandable haughtiness but then he relaxed and began to discuss the various clauses, which were, according to Lawrence, 'in the main agreed to by the chiefs who would themselves supply us with provisions, we agreeing to evacuate the cantonment within three days'. Captain Trevor and Moosa Khan were each made over as hostage to the other side. Mohammed Akbar Khan at first asked for Lawrence but MacNaghten said he could not be spared. At that moment shots began whistling over the heads of the party and a body of horsemen could be seen advancing but were checked, presumably on the orders of the chiefs, who may indeed have ordained the incident, although as events were to show they did not have much control over the Ghilzais. The conference then broke up with mutual assurances of friendship and good faith; although Lawrence was to write, 'The chiefs' specious courtesy to us was all assumed, with a view to veiling their ulterior treacherous designs and removing any suspicions we might have.' He was, of course, writing with the benefits of hindsight.

Akbar Khan.

Meanwhile the troops at the Bala Hissar were ordered to move out and join the force in the cantonment whilst a supply of ammunition was sent to Shah Shuja's troops and he was told of the terms, that the British were leaving him in the lurch. On 16 December therefore the 54th Regiment and a troop of horse artillery marched out and were fired at all the way by Ghilzais. Meanwhile, despite the treaty stipulation, which the British assumed to have been accepted, no supplies came in. 'Some of our Mohammedan soldiers and our camp followers had to subsist upon carrion,' wrote Lawrence.

MacNaghten now contacted the chiefs who said they did not

trust the British to withdraw so long as they retained hold of the magazine and the Masjid, Rhikhab Bashee and Zulfikar Khan's forts; and that they could not help until these had been evacuated. For once, even the General demurred and MacNaghten urged that the troops should march out at once in order of battle and enter Kabul, or fight beneath its walls. Elphinstone's brief flash of soldierly pride was insufficient for this and once again he declined to take adventurous action, so the forts were given up. The Envoy and Lawrence watched from a mound, accompanied by the hostage Moosa Khan, an old man 'who evidently sympathised with us and participated in the feelings of shame and anguish it was in vain for either of us to stifle or conceal'.

Inevitably, instead of being conciliated by the surrender of the forts, the enemy now raised their demands and on 20 December at another meeting, attended by Mackenzie and Lawrence with the Envoy, the chiefs demanded the surrender of the 9-pounder guns, which was rejected by MacNaghten, who, on their return to the cantonment, urged the General to break off all negotiations as futile and vain and 'to take our chance in the field as he felt sure we would beat them if we only marched out boldly and met the rebels in the open plain'; but, according to Lawrence, the General, supported by the senior officers around him, repeated that retreat was the only solution.

The chiefs now returned to the issue of hostages as security for the safe evacuation of the force and Captains Conolly, and Airey, ADC to Elphinstone, volunteered to join Trevor, who had been a hostage since the 11th, whose wife pleaded for his return – with disastrous consequences as it turned out. In addition to Conolly and Airey, Skinner and Drummond, who had been concealed in the city since the outbreak, were now in Afghan hands. They already had four officers – the number originally demanded.

The next day, at yet another conference, it was disclosed that a letter had been intercepted to an Indian banker in Kabul, requesting his help for the British. This time the chiefs behaved in an overbearing manner and not only omitted the usual courtesies, but also failed to dismount when talking. Referring to the letter, they spoke of treachery and breach of faith by the

British, although the Envoy explained that it had been written by Major Leach at Khalat-i-Ghilzi who was unaware of the current negotiations.

Hitherto, MacNaghten had been scrupulously correct in rejecting overtures from individual chiefs whilst negotiating with them as a body but now realized that even when acting collectively they failed to observe agreements and decided that this policy would get him nowhere. Consequently, he decided to treat separately with Mohammed Akbar Khan. This was the worst step he could have taken, for Akbar, despite his courage, occasional chivalry and generosity of spirit, was too volatile, too devious and too self-centred for such a role.

On 21 December the hostages were finally decided on. They were to be Airey, Pottinger, Warburton and Conolly and were to start at once for the city. For some reason Walsh and Webb were also sent. All were junior officers except for Major Pottinger. The next day, Captain Skinner, who had been a prisoner on parole in the city since 2 November, arrived in the company of Sirdat Selim Khan, Akbar's cousin, with proposals from Akbar. These were that Shah Shuja should remain on his throne with Akbar as his chief minister; that the British troops in the Bala Hissar and Mohammed Sherreef's fort should remain until the spring; and that Amenullah Khan, the instigator of the uprising, should be surrendered to the British. Strangely, MacNaghten rejected the last proposal, seeing in it perhaps some local paying-off of scores. However, he thought that the other suggestions formed a reasonable basis for a meeting the following day.

On 23 December, therefore, the negotiators moved off, including MacNaghten, Trevor, Mackenzie and Lawrence, with an escort of ten troopers. The Envoy seemed to be uncharacteristically excited in manner but nevertheless, when at the last minute the General expressed his fear that there was treachery afoot, MacNaghten declined to turn back. He replied that even so, he would still prefer to march out to do battle instead of negotiating; but Elphinstone answered, 'MacNaghten, I can't; the troops are not to be depended on.'

As they moved off through a crowd of Afghans with jezzails and long knives, congregated at the gate, Lawrence noted that the reserve guard had not been ordered out to be ready for any emergency. MacNaghten agreed that it was remiss of Elphinstone and Shelton not to have any troops ready, adding, 'But it is of a piece with all the rest.' Lawrence rode back to order the remainder of the Envoy's escort to join them, before catching up with his companions.

Some days before, Mohammed Akbar Khan (hereafter referred to as Akbar) had asked to receive as presents Lawrence's pair of double-barrelled pistols and Captain Grant's charger. The pistols had been reluctantly sent to him but the horse, which had been forgotten, was not sent for to join the party. Sir William gave orders to Lawrence to ride to the Bala Hissar to tell Shah Shuja of the outcome of the conference when it had been concluded. He knew as well as any of them that treachery was possible, but when warned of it, replied, 'Of course there is but what can I do? The General has declared his inability to fight, we have no prospect of aid from any quarter, the enemy are only playing with us . . .'

When the little party reached the appointed place, 300 yards from the cantonment, they found Akbar awaiting them, with Mohammed Shah Khan, Sultan Jan and other Ghilzai chiefs. Salutations of 'Peace be with you' were exchanged and Grant's horse handed over. Akbar expressed his thanks for it as well as for Lawrence's pistols, which he was wearing. They all dismounted and sat on horse rugs spread on a small mound free of snow, Trevor and Mackenzie seated beside the Envoy. Lawrence stood behind him but when asked to be seated by Akbar, he knelt on one knee. The escort was drawn up a short distance in the rear. Lawrence pointed out the unusually large number of Afghans gathered round to the Envoy who commented on this to Akbar who replied, 'Oh we are all in the same boat and Lawrence Sahib need not be in the least alarmed. As soon as these words were spoken the pistols were snatched from Lawrence's waist, his sword drawn from its scabbard and his arms pinioned by Mohammed Shah Khan who raised him up from the ground, saying 'If you value your life come along with me.' At that moment Lawrence turned to see Sir William, head facing down the slope, wrists locked in the grip of Akbar; and

Trevor and Mackenzie in much the same state. Seeing that resistance was useless, he told Mohammed Shah Khan to lead on. All this happened in less time than it takes to read these lines. Swarms of Afghans now crowded round Lawrence claiming him as a sacrifice to their vengeance, but were kept off by Mohammed Shah Khan's retinue who closed in and fought all round him. They made for the horses where Lawrence was ordered to mount behind Mohammed Shah Khan. He drove his spurs into his horse in order to keep him on his feet if he fell on the slippery frozen snow which would mean certain death. Mohammed Akbar Khan's guards were still all round him but were, in his own words, 'keeping off with great difficulty the savages yelling for my blood and receiving themselves many blows intended for me'. Oddly enough, many of the assailants were also retainers of Mohammed Shah Khan, who were only restrained from firing by the danger of hitting their chief. Nevertheless, they continued to keep striking Lawrence with the butts of their firelocks and their long swords, shouting 'Drop the infidel. Why spare the accursed – let us shed the Kafir's blood.'[1]

Despite these attentions, Lawrence was safely borne through the mêlée to Mohammed Sherreef's fort at whose gates a large body of horsemen were drawn up, opening their ranks only to admit their chief and his men. Meanwhile Mackenzie had a similar experience. He had had a presentiment of disaster and only dismounted unwillingly. Almost immediately he saw Akbar and his cousin Sultan Jan lay hands on the Envoy before he was pinioned and surrounded by Ghilzais. Mackenzie was lifted up behind one of the Afghans who rode through a mob of tribesmen yelling, 'Kill the Kafir' and was taken to a dungeon in the same fort where he was locked in with Lawrence.

Poor Trevor had fared much worse, for although he was also mounted behind a chief the horse fell on the ice and he was cut to pieces by inflamed tribesmen. Mackenzie's horse had also fallen but fortunately it had happened just before they reached the gate of the fort and he was saved by a chief who fell on top of him covering him from the mob. They had now discovered the whereabouts of the two officers and began spitting through the bars of the dark ground-floor cell, cursing them and calling on the guards to release them, holding up the heads of several Britons they had decapitated and a human hand which turned out to be one of MacNaghten's. A blunderbus was pushed through the bars and the prisoners were only saved by a guard who pushed it up at the moment of firing.

Several chiefs who now came to see them assured them that the Envoy and Trevor were safe. Either they were deliberately lying to reduce the officers' morale when they learnt the truth or possibly they themselves did not know and were only following the time-honoured custom of the East in saying what the other person wants to hear. But there was no sort of civility when they were followed by Amenullah Khan who, according to Lawrence's account, addressed them 'in the most savage manner, assuring us that he would have us both blown away from the guns'. After him came several mullahs to say that if an attack was made on the fort they would both be put to death. They forced Lawrence to write to Elphinstone to tell him to carry out the plan for retreat and not try to come to the captives' assistance. Later on the Mullahs returned with the note, saying that it was unnecessary to give it to Elphinstone who was obviously not going to attack and had freed all captured Afghans. An exception to all this threatening behaviour was provided by one old mullah who denounced the chiefs as a disgrace to Islam. Whether this alternation between kind and harsh behaviour, as practised in modern methods of interrogation, was planned or not, will never be known. Probably it was not, for throughout the story of the hostages there were many examples of kindness contrasting with hostility.

Lawrence and Mackenzie were given sheepskin cloaks and shared a meal with their captors before falling asleep. They were woken at midnight when they were again mounted on horses behind chiefs who rode through the deserted city streets to Akbar's house where he received them courteously, lamenting the day's events and even affecting to shed tears. They were then taken to another room where they found Skinner and learnt for the first time of the deaths of MacNaghten and Trevor. Skinner had seen the Envoy's head brought into the courtyard. Apparently he had resisted when Akbar had told him to get up from the blanket, pushing Akbar away. At that moment someone cried out that the British were advancing and in panic Akbar shot MacNaghten. This was the story as Skinner had heard it and is probably true for with MacNaghten in his hands Akbar would have had a considerable bargaining asset. When he and his men rode off, the Ghilzais mutilated the corpse, dragging it through the city and sticking the head up in Char Chowk, the most frequented and open part of the city.

Lawrence thought that MacNaghten had fallen victim to his high sense of honour in rejecting Shah Shuja's proposals to execute certain chiefs known to be treacherous: 'When through the imbecility of the military authorities, the Envoy was compelled, sorely against his will and his own judgement, to enter into negotiations with the hostile chiefs, he behaved with consummate prudence and strictly fulfilled to the very letter his own part of the engagements entered into with them, although every stipulation was evaded and every promise deliberately broken on their part.' Lawrence reiterated that it was only because he seemed unable to negotiate with the chiefs as a body that he had turned to Akbar partly because his father and family were prisoners of the British, partly because of Akbar's known enmity with Amenullah Khan, the leader of the revolt. Of MacNaghten, Lawrence wrote, 'Many a brave man has fallen in his country's cause but no braver or more devoted servant of the state ever sacrificed his life in the execution of his duty than my beloved and ever-to-be lamented chief.'

It was a gloomy Christmas Eve for the British. Lady Sale had the onerous task of informing Lady MacNaghten and Mrs Trevor of their husbands' murders. 'Over such scenes I draw a veil,' she wrote. Lawrence and Mackenzie were sent for again by Akbar, who referred to them as his 'honoured guests' and suggested that they should adopt Afghan dress. Despite doing so they were recognized on their return ride and the escort had to close round them as the crowd were baying for their blood.

This time they were taken to the house of Zeman Khan where they found Conolly and Airey and many of the principal chiefs in conference. All professed sorrow at the death of MacNaghten. 'They had the audacity,' wrote Lawrence, 'to blame him for not having fulfilled the terms submitted by him on the 9th December, totally forgetting that they themselves had rendered the agreement a dead letter...' At this meeting a new draft agreement was drawn up to which the prisoners were not allowed to suggest any modification. It was demanded that all the ladies should be made over as hostages; but when the four British officers demurred 'that such a proposal,' according to Lawrence, 'was utterly abhorrent to our feelings and at variance with our custom', this was shelved for the time being.

One of these ladies, Florentia Sale, wrote a few days later that the Council of War, consisting of Elphinstone, Shelton, Anquetil and Chambers, together with Pottinger, had ratified this treaty.

Lady Sale.

Scornfully she wrote, 'No-one but themselves exactly knows what this treaty is; further than that it is most disgraceful! 14½ lakhs to be given for our safe conduct to Peshawar, all our guns to be given up except six; and six hostages to be given on our part; and when they are sent, Lawrence and Mackenzie are to return.' Shortly afterwards, Lawrence did return, looking, according to Lady Sale, 'haggard and ten years older from anxiety', and recounted all that had happened. He had heard that the Envoy's body was hanging from a tree and his head kept in a bag in the chowk, from where Akbar was going to send it to Bokhara to show the king there how he had seized the Feringhees here and what he meant to do with them. Lady Sale finished by writing, prophetically, 'Whether we go by treaty or not, I fear but few of us will live to reach the provinces.'

Lady Sale had earlier heard of the murders and proposed treaty from Lawrence whilst he was still a prisoner and had been forced to send to the General the copy of the treaty, sealed by Mohammed Zeman Khan, Amenullab Khan and Osman Khan (but not by Akbar who may have been keeping his options open) and Lawrence managed to send a note with it to Lady Sale with another of condolence to Mrs Trevor and a note from Conolly to Lady MacNaghten. Thus Florentia Sale had advance notice of the treaty provisions, of the handing over of the 'treasure', guns and ammunition.

After this and before Lawrence returned to the cantonment on the 29th he and Mackenzie returned to Akbar's house, where they were treated well enough although Akbar's confidential servant, Moosah Khan, remained in the room next door to ensure that they had no contacts with the outside world. However, they were able to see Skinner again and learnt of his escape on 2 November when the uprising began. At 7 o'clock Mr Baness, an Indian merchant who had just arrived with stores for the officers, rushed into Skinner's house to tell him to ride fast for the cantonment. Unfortunately, as he was waiting for his horse to be brought round, a mob approached the house. He just had time to put on Afghan dress and escape through a side door into the compound of an adjoining house where an old lady rapidly slipped a boorkha over him and a veil over his head.

He spent a month there disguised as a woman. The family treated him with such kindness that after a month he insisted on being handed over so that his protectors should come to no harm. They only agreed to give him up after extracting a promise from the Afghans that his life should be spared.

On Christmas Day Akbar visited his captives, bringing one of the pistols which Lawrence had reluctantly given him, at the Envoy's suggestion, as one of the locks was out of order and he was required to put it right. Both barrels had been discharged and Akbar made out that he had fired them at Ghilzais. Lawrence wrote, 'The truth was that this false traitor had fired them at MacNaghten and stained his hand with a foul and treacherous murder. I felt quite sick at the thought and returned his weapon to the assassin without further remark, but with the deepest loathing and abhorrence.' Another visitor was Sultan Jan who 'inveighed most bitterly against our occupation of his country and the indignities to which his countrymen, and women especially, had been subjected by our troops and by some of our officers who he named'. In this respect the Afghans had a genuine grievance which Lawrence did not try to gainsay.

On Boxing Day letters arrived at the cantonment with the news that relieving forces had reached Peshawar but had been defeated at the Khyber and forced to retreat. Lady Sale thought that even if they were successful they could not arrive in time 'to save us from either a disgraceful treaty or a disastrous retreat'. Her military prescience was proved only too correct for in the end both treaty and retreat were equally disgraceful. If only this indomitable lady who had for years followed the drum as a soldier's wife, had been the General in place of poor old Elphinstone . . .

Back in the city that day, Lawrence was summoned to Amenullah Khan's house rejecting Mackenzie's offer to go with him, saying 'we should neither of us rush heedless into danger but each take his own turn as circumstances might require.' He wrote that 'It was no wonder that both of us felt a shrinking from appearing in the presence of such a monster of cruelty as Akbar Khan who would not hesitate a moment to torture and put us to death, so utter was his contempt for human life . . .' Nevertheless

Lawrence, who had often met him at the Envoy's and in the presence of Shah Shuja, was received courteously. Amenullah Khan told Lawrence that Elphinstone and Pottinger had asserted that bills could not be drawn on India for the money stipulated in the new treaty unless Lawrence, who had the authority of the late Envoy, could prepare them 'in regular form'.

He was put in a room to do this and in the evening was again sent for to attend another meeting with Amenullah Khan and other chiefs, who all rose when he entered the room. Amenullah Khan opened the proceedings by first praising MacNaghten and then accusing him of offering Akbar two lakhs of rupees for his head. Lawrence denied this but did admit that the Envoy had considered arresting Amenullah Khan as the leader of the revolt and keeping him confined. Nevertheless he insisted that the Envoy was incapable of bribing anyone to commit murder and in any case he, Lawrence, as the Envoy's confidential secretary, would have known about it and could therefore swear that there had been no such arrangement.

The chiefs now renewed their earlier demand for the women and children to be made over to them as hostages, which Lawrence again said was quite impossible. They also mentioned the names of suitable officers to be hostages, including Macgregor, the political agent in Jelalabad and a Sergeant Dean, who had been involved in monetary transactions. Lawrence told them that the sergeant was not an officer and Amenullah Khan said, 'Lawrence sahib is truthful and to be depended on, he might easily have passed off Dean to us as an officer fit for a hostage, but he would not deceive us. We shall trust him. He is a man of truth.' Instead, other officers were named, including Captain Conolly, assistant political agent and commander of the Envoy's escort, Captain Drummond of the 3rd Light Cavalry, Captain Airey, an ADC, Captains Walsh and Webb of the Shah's sappers and Warburton of the Shah's artillery, all of whom were already in their hands. Lawrence was returned to his room where he got little sleep as his guards pestered him with questions most of the night.

On the 27th he had another long interview with Amenullah Khan and was given presents of fruit and sweetmeats; and on the

28th he managed to contact a friendly Kashmiri merchant, formerly employed by Burnes, who told him that Akbar had opposed his release in a conference of chiefs but that Amenullah Khan had pledged his word to free him but not Mackenzie. Accordingly, he gave Lawrence three criminals to carry his goods and sent him on his way with a message to Elphinstone to avoid the Khoord Kabul passes, which were under Akbar's control.

At 5 o'clock the next morning Lawrence set out, dressed as an Afghan, his face covered by half of his turban, except for one eye, with an escort of 100 men under command of Amenullah Khan's son. They halted within gunshot of the cantonment before Lawrence went forward followed by three men and yaboos containing his goods. When challenged by the sentry, he replied that he was Captain Lawrence, to which the man stammered out, 'Oh Sir, welcome a thousand times. We never thought to have seen you again.'

After meeting Elphinstone and Pottinger he visited the ladies, writing of it later, 'My meeting with poor Lady MacNaghten and Mrs Trevor was so heartrending that I cannot venture to describe it.' His old Hindu bearer wept for joy and many of the sepoys of the 37th and others of the escort crowded round him rejoicing at his escape. He learnt that when they were forced to withdraw to the cantonment, a Rajput jemadar rushed forward, sword in hand, and was cut to pieces. The mêlée in which the Envoy had been killed must have been seen from the cantonment, yet no-one was sent forward to find out what had happened: no reconnaissance, no sortie, 'not even a gun fired'. Nor was there any attempt to recover the bodies which were visible through field glasses. 'Thus', wrote Lawrence, 'almost within musket shot of our entrenched position and in broad day, a British Envoy had been barbarously murdered and his mangled body allowed to remain for hours where he fell . . .'

Sturt told Lawrence that he had urged the General to attack Mahommed Khan's fort with two regiments and that very night to move off for Jelalabad. Pottinger had agreed and had urged Elphinstone to put himself at the head of the troops, who were by now so inflamed that they would have stormed into the city. Admittedly, the men of the garrison were not certain of what had happened and who had been killed but it was obvious when the remnants of the escort returned that something drastic had happened. Elphinstone had instead sent a message to all commanding officers to say that the Envoy and his aides were safe and had been taken to Mohammed Khan's to protect them from the tribesmen – a half truth that omitted the murders. The next day, however, Lawrence's letters arrived and the whole camp was made aware of the true horror of the circumstances.

According to Lawrence's version of events, Afghan treachery was now so apparent that Pottinger remonstrated against holding any more treaty negotiations and urged instead that the army should either march on the Bala Hissar for the winter or make straight for Jelalabad unaccompanied by baggage or stores. 'Such was the infatuation of our military leaders,' wrote Lawrence, 'that even though information of the despatch of an army from India to our aid had reached us, they determined to reject both proposals and accept the treaty proposed by the Afghans. They bound themselves also, contrary to Pottinger's most vehement protest, to pay to the enemy 12½ lakhs for a safe conduct to Peshawar . . .'

The treaty read '. . . An agreement of peace determined on with the Frank English gentlemen' and went on to stipulate the return to India of all British forces from Kabul, Ghazni, Kandahar and Jelalabad. Dost Mohammed was to be restored, the remaining cash in the treasury (much had been looted from Johnson's house) to be handed over as well as all guns except six to be retained by the retreating force. Finally there was a clause, 'If any of the Frank gentlemen had taken a Mussulman wife she shall be given up.' This was obviously aimed at Warburton but was not complied with for the good reason that no-one knew of her whereabouts. Fortunately, not all the conditions of this shameful document were adhered to and the garrisons in other parts of the country remained where they were.

Although Lawrence had prepared the bills on India for the cash demanded, he had insisted that they should be cashed only on presentation of certificates from the political agent in Peshawar, certifying that the army had arrived safety, thus preventing the bills from being marketable in Kabul.

On the 29th and 30th Warburton, Drummond, Walsh and Webb, who had been allowed back into the cantonment, were returned to Kabul, with their assent, to be hostages, together with the sick and wounded under a subaltern of the 44th, with Doctors Berwick and Campbell. On their way to the city most of their baggage and bedding was plundered by the crowd surging around.

Provisions and cattle were brought into the camp, although quite often potential sellers were robbed at the gates. Shelton had said that there should be no firing, so the taunts thrown at the soldiers went unchecked and discipline became even worse. Even some of the Afghan chiefs had urged that the troops should fire on the marauders; but Elphinstone had made up his mind to offer no provocation to anyone and to retreat as soon as possible by the Khoord Kabul passes, ignoring Amenullah Khan's advice.

On New Year's Eve 1841, Lawrence wrote, 'Thus sadly closed this miserable year.' The next day there was a heavy fall of snow, making all the sepoys look cold and miserable. Knowing that the British were on their way out, crowds of Afghans around the gates were bartering curiosities in exchange for baggage, which had to be lightened. Lawrence gave his cocked hat to one fellow, 'who instantly clapped it on his head and galloped off to the city, narrowly escaping being shot by his friends'. Even now, however, there were many Afghans who could not believe that the British would really leave their position. On the other hand 'native' officers of Anderson's Horse brought alarming reports and said that the only possible course now was for the troops to march rapidly, sacrificing stragglers and all baggage. They also said that Akbar had made them offers to go over to him – which, in due course they did. Had Elphinstone acted on their advice, instead of taking no notice, this may not have happened.

On 2 January a message came to the force from Kohistanis offering to escort the British to Peshawar, even offering to give hostages as a sign of good faith. But this, like everything else, was ignored. Lawrence received a message from Shah Shuja warning the British not to leave the cantonment as no trust could be placed in the chiefs' promises; but this also was ignored, even though the Shah had warned that so long as they stayed where they were, there was hope, but as soon as they moved out they were as good as dead. A similar message came from a Kuzzilbash chief, on which no action was taken. The Gaddarene swine were determined to rush over the edge, come what may.

Lady Sale, who had written that the chiefs were dictating to them, delaying the departure of the force, 'which is to be postponed according to their pleasure', noted that although the Nawab Zeman Shah Khan, Osman Khan and Mohammed Shah Khan all appeared to be honourable men, no-one seemed able to control the Ghilzais, who had stolen the camels taking the wounded to Kabul and had then returned only inferior beasts.

On 2 January she wrote, 'We hear from the city that Sale [as she always referred to her husband] has been taking forts, carrying off women and provisions and greatly annoying the good people of Jelalabad . . .' He had been given deliberately ambiguous orders, putting all the onus on him for whatever transpired. Lady Sale quite understood his situation, writing 'He is, if he can leave his sick and wounded and baggage in perfect safety, to return to Kabul without endangering the force under his command. Now, if Sale succeeds and all is right, he will doubtless be a very fine fellow but if he meets with a reverse, he will be told, "You were not to come up unless you could do so safely." ' No wonder he chose to stay put and do as much damage as possible to the enemy from where he was.

On 6 January 4,500 troops and 12,000 camp followers, struggled out into the snow, their leaders absurdly confident that Akbar would keep his word and ensure their safe passage, Lawrence gave a vivid description of this march: 'At 9 a.m. the troops moved off, a crouching, drooping, dispirited army, so different from the smart, light-hearted body of men they appeared some time ago.' No Afghan was to be seen as they left, slowly picking their way through the snow, sinking a foot deep at every step on the main track and several feet if they came off it. 'As we crossed the Seah Sung hills and threaded our way through our old and once jovial camp, now so silent and deserted, my heart sank within me at the remembrance of the past, and under the conviction that we were a doomed force.' Looking at the Bala

Hissar, Lawrence thought that even at that late hour they could have got there. 'I strove to drive away these melancholy and desponding forebodings by riding as hard as my powerful horse, one belonging to the late Envoy, could carry me from the head to the rear of my charge [of the Envoy's escort and the civilians] striving by an assumed air of cheerfulness to encourage the poor, terrified women and children.' When they had gone a short way they were ordered to halt and retrace their steps as the chiefs had said they were not yet ready to escort them. Fortunately the General thought that it was too late to turn back and the march continued after an hour halted in the bitter cold.

Among the group of women and children in his charge was Lady Sale, who had confided to her diary two days before, 'The Afghans still tell us that we are doomed and warn us to be particularly cautious of our safety in going out of cantonments.' She did not agree with Lawrence that the Bala Hissar could still have been attained: 'How are we to get our ammunition in?' wrote this acerbic General's wife a day or two before when the proposal had again been raised to 'erect a battery on the Siah Sung hill (of course to be the work of fairies during the night)'. She had heard from Sale again on the 4th that an advance guard of cavalry as well as the 3rd Buffs, six regiments of N.I., artillery and sappers had arrived at Jelalabad, with three months' pay overdue; and anticipated no relief from that quarter, hoping that the Kandahar force, which had not been mauled at all, might save them but he was unaware of any movement on that front. Everyone suffered from poor communications and the fog of rumour. For this reason Sale had been sending extracts from his wife's letters to the Commander-in-Chief back in India, as no-one else had any idea of what was happening in Afghanistan. Some of her more trenchant letters may, from now on, perhaps have been influenced by this knowledge but it is doubtful if she could have behaved in any other way, given her nature and experience of army life.

Meanwhile, the 'army' struggled on. The advance guard consisted of HM's 44th of Foot, the 4th Irregular Horse, Skinner's Horse, two artillery 6-pounders, some sappers and miners, the mountain train and the former Envoy's escort. The main body was composed of the 5th and 37th N.I., the latter guarding the 'treasure' – what was left of it – Anderson's Horse, the Shah's 6th Regiment and two Horse Artillery 6-pounders. In the rearguard were the 54th N.I., the 5th Cavalry and the two Horse Artillery 6-pounders. The ladies and children were placed with the advance guard in the charge of the Envoy's escort under Lawrence; but Lady Sale and her daughter-in-law, Mrs Sturt, rode mixed up with the troops of the Irregular Horse as they had been advised to do, presumably to be less conspicuous.

Lawrence found it difficult to keep his charge together as some of the bearers were hurrying on whilst others lagged behind with the palanquins and doolies containing most of the women and children. They had only covered four miles before halting for the night. No camp had been marked out and there were only a few tents, pitched for the women, most of whom, however, remained in the doolies and palanquins for greater warmth. Three of Lawrence's servants had caught up with him and 'these faithful men, instead of caring for themselves', did everything they could to make him comfortable, clearing a space and pitching a tent. He and two other officers crept into it, grateful for the sherry and cold meat given them by Lady Sale. Mackenzie was one of the few other officers of this demoralized force to have the wit to adapt to the conditions. He and his few Jezzailchees cleared a space in the snow that night, covered it with their posteens and lay in a tight-packed circle with their feet in the centre. The next day Mackenzie said they had hardly felt the cold.

That day, 7 January, John Conolly wrote to Mackenzie from Kabul to say that hundreds of wounded and frost-bitten sepoys had made their way into the city. They heard that the rearguard, which should have left at midday, did not set out until three in the afternoon and had had to leave the luggage and spike the guns. They were attacked as soon as they left and had suffered a number of casualties. Crowds of Afghans had rushed into the cantonment and plundered everything they could get hold of. As they started out there was total confusion with crowds of camp followers and herds of cattle all mixed up together. By the time they reached the bank of the canal it was so slippery that it was impassable for the camels. They had had to fight all the way, passing through 'a continuous line of poor wretches, men, women and children, dead or dying from the cold or wounds, who, unable to move, entreated their comrades to kill them and put them out of their misery'. Although he was not himself part of the rearguard, there is no reason to doubt the accuracy of Lawrence's description. They did not make camp until midnight, when they found no shelter, food or fuel prepared for them. They could only huddle together in the snow, their silent stillness betraying their despair. The next morning Lawrence found near his tent an elderly British warrant officer, in full regimentals, sword in hand, who had lain down to die.

Even the advance guard, leaving at 9 o'clock, had made very slow progress as there was only one small bridge over a nullah, only eight feet wide but very deep. Lady Sale wrote:

> Great stress had been laid on the necessity of a bridge over the Kabul river, about half a mile from cantonments . . . in vain had Sturt represented over and over again, that as the river was perfectly fordable, it was a labour of time and inutility: with the snow a foot deep the men must get their feet wet. However, as usual every sensible proposition was over-ruled and Sturt was sent long before daylight to make the bridge with gun carriages and they could not be placed overnight as the Afghans would have carried them off; he had therefore to work for hours up to his hips in water with the comfortable assurance that when his unprofitable task was finished he could not hope for dry clothes until the end of March, and immediately on quitting the water they were all frozen stiff. I do not mention this as an individual grievance but to show the inclemency of the weather and the general misery sustained.

Only as they moved slowly onwards was it realized that the bullocks could not draw gun carriages through the snow. As Sturt had predicted, the bridges proved unnecessary for the troops as the river was quite fordable. His wife rode through it with the horsemen but the poor camp followers, scared of going into the water, did use the bridge on which they jostled for turns. As a result there was not only a long delay but much of the baggage and commissariat stores were lost. The followers could hardly be blamed for their panic, for whereas the troops had at least been on half rations, they had had to exist on what meat they could find from dead animals and were suffering from malnutrition even before they set out. Nor were they able to keep warm as the chiefs had forbidden the cutting down of any more trees and there was a scarcity of firewood. For their dinner and breakfast before setting out, Lady Sale and Mrs Sturt had utilised the wood of their dining table to cook on.

When the rearguard were fired on as they left the cantonment many of the servants threw away their loads. The only baggage saved of the Sales was Mrs Sturt's bedding on which the Ayah[2] sat when riding. They had to scrape sleeping places out of the snow on that intensely cold first night and they had no food except a small amount of bhoosa they had purchased. That night there were many desertions, including most of the Shah's 6th Regiment.

At 7.30 the next morning, leaving behind the men who had frozen to death during the night, the force set out, although no orders were given or bugle blown. Many of the sepoys and followers had just pushed on and Lady Sale wrote, 'Discipline was clearly at an end.' There must have been some semblance of staff work for the roles of advance and rearguard were reversed, but Lawrence endorsed Lady Sale's comments on discipline, writing 'Already all discipline and order had ceased and soldiers, camp followers and baggage were all mixed up together.'

Sepoys were throwing away their muskets which were too cold to handle and most of the Shah's troops had now returned to Kabul. Lawrence's command of the women and children and Envoy's escort remained unmolested, although by now there were hundreds of enemy horse and foot encroaching on each flank, ostensibly as the escort provided by the chiefs. Unfortunately some of the bearers of the palanquins and doolies were so tired that they could not go on. Lawrence, therefore, mounted Lady MacNaghten in front of him and rode up the column looking for alternative transport. At last he found a camel with empty kajawahs, lifting her into one, balancing the other with bundles of clothes. He then rode back down the column, only to find his charges mixed up with the remnants of Brigadier Anquetil's rearguard. The Afghans had sallied out from a fort and captured the mountain guns, due to the misconduct of the 44th who had been the escort. Their Adjutant had been wounded whilst ineffectually trying to rally the men, and Anquetil, who said this incident was 'too bad to speak about', sent Troup to get help from the 37th N.I. who proved, literally, too worn out to do anything. Lawrence considered this to be true, 'for this gallant regiment never shrank from duties, was ever forward and an example to the army, never refusing to face a foe whenever called upon'. Major Swayne of the 5th N.I. then led a charge at the head of a few men of his unit but it was too late and the enemy carried off the guns.

The night which Lawrence had spent in a tent with others, and Mackenzie laagered up with his men, Lady Sale and Mrs Sturt had also been in a tent. There were other people in it, all touching, including Lieutenant Mein of her husband's old regiment, for whom Lady Sale had a soft spot. He had been wounded at Jelalabad and had been sent to the cooler climate of Kabul to convalesce before the insurrection. Lady Sale was furious about all the stop-starts they had endured, writing 'By these unnecessary halts we diminished our provisions; and having no cover for officers and men, they are perfectly paralysed with cold.' She was scornful about the poor old General, with whom 'evil counsels' had prevailed. The column had turned into a shambles and, in her words, most of 'The Sipahees (sic) were mixed up with the camp followers and knew not where to find the headquarters of their corps.' To add to the general misery, the snow was a foot deep and

> There was no food for man or beast . . . numbers of unfortunates have dropped, benumbed with cold, to be massacred by the enemy; yet so bigoted are our rulers that we are still told that the Sirdars are faithful, that Akbar Khan is our friend etc and the reason they wish us to delay is that they may send their troops to clear the passes for us! That they will send them there can be no doubt; but everything is occurring just as was foretold to us before we set out.

Before this second day ended they were attacked by a party of Afghan horsemen who charged into the column, going off with camels and baggage.

As night began to fall on the second day of this massacre, Akbar sent Moosa Khan to summon Skinner and Lawrence to join him. Lawrence, conscious of his obligation to the women and children, declined to go but Skinner went and was told that the army should never have left before their Afghan escort was ready. Akbar demanded another six hostages, to ensure that the troops did not go beyond Tezeen until Jelalabad had been evacuated. Skinner was sent back with this ultimatum for Elphinstone. The enemy had now stopped firing on them for the night; and Lawrence again shared a tent with fellow officers, grateful for some food given by Lady MacNaghten. He and his friends were fortunate to have some cover as the temperature was now 10 degrees below zero. The soldiers and others had to lie on the snow, without food or fuel. Lawrence wrote, 'Who can adequately describe the horror and sufferings of such a situation?' There were frozen corpses everywhere and the enemy were heard all around, just waiting for daylight before attacking again.

A cask of spirits had earlier been broached by some of the British artillerymen to keep up morale and some were now so drunk that they wanted to charge the enemy, although nothing came of it. A number of officers made great efforts to rally their men and before evening some of the 44th had driven off the encroaching enemy and had taken up position on the heights above the force. Lady Sale and her daughter-in-law had sat on their horses for hours with bullets 'whizzing' past them, 'For myself,' wrote Lady Sale of that day, 'whilst I sat for hours on my horse in the cold, I felt very grateful for a tumbler of sherry, which at any other time, would have made me very unladylike but now merely warmed me up . . .'

Even during this shuffling shambles the troops had still been able to respond to good officers. The counter-attack by the 44th had been the product of Major Thain's leadership and Lawrence also had played a courageous part. He had left his charges, having found them all places on camel kajawahs in order to ride back to the rear where he met Captain Anderson of the Irregular Horse who called out, 'The enemy are upon us: have you any of the escort ready?' Lawrence rode back and ordered the subadar of the infantry sections of the Envoy's escort, 'a fine brave old soldier', to close the men round the ladies whilst he rode off with the cavalry element towards the firing. He found the 44th drawn up and the enemy taking long shots at them, creeping towards the brow of the hill where the British soldiers were. Lawrence drew his men up on the right of the 44th, attacking when the 44th charged, the enemy fleeing behind a hillock. Lawrence's men said they would follow him anywhere; and there was still something of this spirit in certain units. 'Even at this, the 11th hour', he wrote, 'we might, if properly led, have driven the enemy like sheep into Kabul and ourselves have occupied the Bala Hissar.' Instead, he was sent for by Elphinstone who told him that Akbar had demanded that he and Shelton, as well as six others, should be handed over as hostages. Pottinger, although wounded, offered to take his place but another message arrived, demanding Lawrence. The General reluctantly agreed and Lawrence set off with Shelton who soon returned to camp after another messenger came to say that he was not needed after all, but that another officer to be selected by Pottinger was to go. Mackenzie was chosen and he and Lawrence rode off at last after these false starts, escorted by two of Akbar's dependants through crowds of the enemy until they reached the Sirdar, as he now styled himself, seated on the side of a hill. They were offered breakfast, ordered to give up their firearms – a rifle and a pair of pistols in Lawrence's case – but allowed to keep their swords.

Lady Sale called Akbar's latest terms, which included, as well as the persons of the political officers he already knew, no less than 15,000 rupees, 'disgraceful propositions'. Unfortunately, just after Lawrence had gone, a note came from Skinner to say that they should not put themselves in Akbar's hands but should press on rapidly. When the march did resume, at midday on 8 January, she referred to the troops as being in the greatest state of disorganization. The baggage had become mixed up with the advance guard and the camp followers had all pushed ahead of them, in their precipitate flight towards Hindoostan. 'Lady Sale, Mein, Sturt and his wife were also now with the advance guard and Mein was able to show them the spot where the previous October he and General Sale had been wounded when their brigade was attacked on their way from Kabul to Jelalabad.'

They came under heavy fire, Mrs Sturt's pony was wounded in the ear and neck and Lady Sale had a ball in her arm that penetrated her posteen. According to Pottinger, Akbar had been heard, on the edge of this mêlée, shouting to the Ghilzai attackers, 'Slay them' in Pushtu, which few British except Pottinger knew, unlike Persian, known to quite a number, which was the usual method of communication between the British and Afghans. Almost at the same time he was heard to cry 'Cease Fire', in Persian, well aware that this would be understood by his adversaries. During the fighting several of the camels holding ladies still sitting in kajawas were killed, including one holding Mrs Boyd and another carrying Mrs Mainwaring and her infant. In the confusion, with Afghans now right inside the column, Mrs Anderson and her eldest child were both carried off. Mrs Mainwaring tried to mount a pony but as it was already carrying a load, she fell off and continued going forward on foot carrying her child. She was unmolested although her shawl was snatched from her shoulders. Trudging through deep snow, picking her way through the corpses, she managed to catch up with the column which had continued on its way the best it could. She had no chance to change her sodden clothes; nor, for that matter did the other women although few of them had had to tramp through such thick snow. Most had been able to continue riding in some form or other. Lady Sale wrote of Mrs Mainwaring: 'I know from experience that it was many days ere my wet habits became thawed and I can fully appreciate her discomforts.' Also carried off during this dreadful encounter were Mrs Bourke, Mrs Stoker, her son Seymour and Mrs Cunningham, all soldiers' wives, as well as a lone child.

By now the pass was completely blocked with this mass of people and HM's 44th of Foot and the 37th N.I. in the rearguard were under heavy fire. The 44th stood their ground but the poor sepoys of the 37th were almost paralysed with cold: 'to such a degree', according to Lady Sale, 'that no persuasion of their officers could induce them to make any effort to dislodge the enemy'. The enemy were in position on the heights and men were dropping from well-aimed fire whilst the column halted for an hour to let the stragglers get well to the front. Already about

500 soldiers had been killed and many more wounded, including Sturt, of whom Lady Sale wrote, 'I could see by the expression of his countenance that there was no hope.' Dr Bryden (who was to be the lone survivor of this march) did all he could as well as cutting the ball out of Lady Sale's wrist. Sturt was laid on his wife's bedding, suffering from an unquenchable thirst, despite Mein's constant efforts to supply him with water, and suffered agony all night whilst about thirty people including his wife and mother-in-law lay packed in the same tent without being able to turn.

Lawrence and Mackenzie had watched the army's agony from their hilltop. They saw the enemy rush onto the baggage in the rear, although Akbar sent someone to halt it which did have some effect. At noon they had ridden off with Akbar, some Ghilzai chiefs and Sultan Jan, who told them to use their swords if anyone came too close. Halting for half an hour whilst Akbar and Sultan Jan rode forward, ostensibly to stop the carnage, they came across the mangled corpses of camp followers. They were in the centre of a group of about thirty Afghan horsemen when they moved on again, seeing as they did so many sepoys and followers being cut down if they professed to have no money or valuables. The poor creatures cried out to the officers to help, in some cases addressing them by name. Near the centre of the Khoord Kabul pass they saw an abandoned gun and the bodies of two British officers.

Lawrence wrote, 'The Ghilzais had now tasted blood and clearly showing their tigerish nature, became very savage and fierce in their demeanour towards ourselves, demanding that we should be given up to them as a sacrifice, brandishing their long, bloodstained knives in our faces . . .' He had difficulty in restraining himself, keeping his hand on his sword hilt. So threatening became the mob around them that the leader of the escort made them leave the road and shelter unnoticed under an overhanging rock. Whilst there, a wounded soldier of the 44th and the younger child of Captain Boyd, who had become separated from his parents, were brought to their shelter on Akbar's orders.

Another arrival, as it began to snow, was a Mrs Bean, wife of a

Captain F. Boyd.

soldier in HM's 13th Light Infantry, who was in such a bad state that when, in the evening after Sultan Jan had joined them, they started to move off again, Lawrence had great difficulty in getting her up behind Mackenzie on his horse.

With every step they took the signs of carnage increased. Lawrence recognized a sergeant of the 44th lying on the ground and dismounted to try and help him and with the aid of two of Sultan Jan's men, to lift him up, but their task was hopeless. From the nape of his neck to his backbone he had been cut to pieces and they just had to leave him to die, despite the man's plea to be shot. They met numbers of the enemy on horseback and on foot laden with plunder, including a horseman with a little Indian girl sitting behind him. As they passed the Khoord Kabul fort the reflection off the snow was almost blinding until they reached another small fort where a room was cleared and a fire lit; and although there were guards all round they were treated with kindness, the guards sharing their scanty meal with them. Lawrence shared his posteen with little Boyd, Mrs Bean crouched in a corner and the men lay with their feet towards the fire.

When they left the next morning, on horses that had been left unsaddled and unfed, Lawrence took Mrs Bean up behind him and she showered him with blessings for not leaving her 'among these savages', as Sultan Jan had proposed to do. Mackenzie took the wounded soldier behind him and an Afghan had young Boyd in front of him. An hour's ride brought them to the Khoord Kabul fort where Akbar received them graciously, saying, 'I have a proposal to make which reasons of humanity alone prompt me to offer and which, I am well aware may be misconstrued' (this is Lawrence's translation). This was to the effect that after the events of the previous day, the British column no longer offered any protection to women and children, two of whom had already been carried off, and that he was no longer able to control the Ghilzais. Therefore he proposed that the remaining women and children, together with their husbands and any wounded officers, should be made over to his protection and that he would send them under escort to Jelalabad. Skinner was sent back to the column with this proposal, agreed by the other officers, to fetch the new hostages.

They had been having a dreadful time that day, the march being a shambles of followers mixed up with fighting men, many of them mounted on yaboos and camels which they had acquired. Poor Sturt died during the march even though Mrs Trevor had given up her place in a kajawa to make him comfortable; but the uneven motion only hastened his death. Lady Sale wrote, 'We had the sorrowful satisfaction of giving him Christian burial.' According to Lieutenant Eyre, he was the only man to have this privilege. From now on, and in most cases before this the dead lay where they had fallen and their corpses froze to the ground.

That evening the families were taken to the Khoord Kabul fort to avail themselves of Akbar's 'protection'. These included: Lady MacNaghten, Lady Sale, Mrs Sturt, Mrs Boyd and two children – who was overjoyed to be reunited with her other child – and Mrs Anderson and two children, one of whom was an infant ten days old. A third child had been carried off. Others included Mrs Eyre and child, Mrs Waller with one, poor Mrs Trevor and seven, two soldiers' wives, one of whom, Mrs Wade, was an Eurasian. The

Mrs Waller.

men were Captains Waller, Troup who had been wounded, Boyd and Anderson: Lieutenant Eyre, who had also been wounded, Lieutenant Mein, Mr Byley, Sergeant Wade and Jacob, Mackenzie's Christian servant.

Already there were Mrs Burnes and the child, Stoker, who had been rescued from Afghans trying to carry him off, 'Covered, we fear,' wrote Lady Sale, 'with his mother's blood; of her we have no account, nor of Mrs Cunningham.' They learnt that Mrs Anderson's little girl had been taken to Kabul and was lodged with Nawab Zeman Shah Khan where she was well treated.

The whole party was now incarcerated in four small rooms,

about fourteen feet by ten, dark, dirty and with only one small door. At midnight they were each given a mess of boiled rice with a small bowl of ghee (clarified butter). At first, few of the British liked this kind of food but some of them grew to appreciate its nutritional properties. Lawrence 'found it distressing beyond expression to see our countrywomen and their helpless children thus placed in the power of these ruffians but there was no help for it. The extreme suffering of mind and body they had endured since the 5th was apparent in their worn and grief-stricken faces.' Lady MacNaghten had saved her possessions, others had nothing except the clothes they were wearing but each was given a posteen and Lawrence was able to distribute some clothes brought by his faithful servant, amongst the men. Mrs Boyd was delighted to find her little boy but the Andersons were heartbroken at the loss of their daughter. It was in these circumstances that Akbar chose to ask Lawrence to tell the others that they were 'his honoured guests' and that he would escort them safely to Jelalabad as soon as possible. Perhaps he half meant it as he said it for he was not without honour and possessed a number of virtues; but he was too aware of his position of power, in relation to the other chiefs, with so many valuable hostages in his hands, ever to have done such a thing without substantial reward.

Not far away the condition of the 'army' was rapidly deteriorating. That night, the last of all objects that would burn were consigned to the fires. Even so, many of the sepoys were too frozen to get up in the morning. They had been attacked going through the Khoord Kabul pass and had been fired on night and day; but even so there was still something of a column to set out the morning after the hostages had left, with the 44th in the van. Whilst they and some of the 5th Bengal cavalry pushed on to Kubbar-i-Jubbar the main column was ambushed in a narrow defile, only ten feet wide. Brandishing their swords the tribesmen literally cut them up.

Still the march continued the following day with Shelton bringing up the rear with troops who had retained some element of discipline and were able to repel the constant attacks. That evening they reached a ruined fort at Jagdaluk where they received a message from Akbar asking for Elphinstone, Shelton and Johnson to join him, saying that he had tried in vain to call off the Ghilzais, probably insuring himself against the future when the British would return and he could plead 'not guilty'. By now many of the locally recruited and Indian cavalry had deserted, leaving only 55 men of the 44th, their discipline still intact, 26 officers, mostly from Indian or locally recruited units whose men had deserted, as well as 'politicals' and staff officers, 6 British horse artillerymen and a remnant of camp followers. Without their General and despite reluctance to leave dying and wounded comrades to the mercy of the Ghilzais, they kept on their march to certain death.

CHAPTER IV

Hostages and Prisoners

On 11 January the unhappy party set out under escort on the first of many journeys during their nine months of captivity, leaving behind, on their captors' orders, all their servants who were unable to march. Of this, their first walk as prisoners, which was what they really were despite Akbar's protestations that they were his guests, Lady Sale wrote,

> It would be impossible for me to describe the feelings with which we pursued our way through the dreadful scenes that awaited us: the road covered with awfully mangled bodes, all naked; fifty-eight Europeans were counted; the natives were innumerable. Numbers of camp followers still alive, frost-bitten and starving; some perfectly out of their senses and idiotic. Major Ewart, 54th and Major Scott, 44th, were recognised as we passed them, with some others. The sight was dreadful; the smell of blood sickening; and the corpses lay so thick it was impossible to look from them, as it required care to guide my horse so as not to tread upon the bodies...

For the most part, the ladies were in kajawahs on camels and those officers who had been allowed to retain their mounts were on horseback. The soldiers and others just had to trudge along, unable to avoid the sight of the stripped and mangled bodies or of the groups of frostbitten wounded huddled together for a semblance of warmth. To these, in Lawrence's words, 'The boon of death had not yet been granted, and who in hopeless misery and silent despair, saw us pass, well knowing that we could not help or deliver them.' He recognized the body of the 'venerable old Subedar of the Envoy's escort, Appambul Singh, lying on the road by the side of his dun horse'. Lawrence was told that the Afghans had offered him his life if he would go over to them but the old subedar had refused, saying, 'For forty-one years I have eaten the Company's salt.' For sixteen miles they passed through these scenes until reaching Tezeen Fort at sunset.

After a night at Tezeen Fort they set off again on the road taken by the retreating army where the snow was dyed red and they saw, in Eyre's words, 'the mangled bodies of British and Hindoostanee soldiers and helpless camp followers . . .' They passed numerous parties of truculent Ghilzais, the chief perpetrators of those horrors, who passed them laden with booty, their naked swords still reeking with the blood of their victims. 'They uttered deep curses and sanguinary threats at our party and seemed disappointed that so many of the hated Feringhees should have been suffered to survive.'

At Tezeen they had met Lieutenant Melville of the 54th who had been wounded whilst guarding the colours and whose wounds had been dressed by Akbar (to whom he had surrendered) who had made him wear a turban with a posteen over his shoulders, riding with him to help him escape detection – another side of this extraordinary man that he was to show on several occasions.

On their way the next day they were joined by Dr McGrath of the 37th Regiment whom everyone thought had been killed. He had followed a body of Irregular Horse but had not realized until it was too late that they were going over to the enemy. There were also three soldiers of the 44th who had followed him. As the hostages continued along the valley of Tezeen they passed several abandoned horse artillery guns and also saw the body of Dr Cardew, known as the 'Fighting Doctor' and loved by the troops for his kindness as well as his professional skills. They spent the night in bivouac in the snow, the women and children laagered up behind a barrier of Lady MacNaghten's trunks and Lawrence's baggage; they were glad of tea and sherry from his and Lady MacNaghten's stocks.

The following day they kept on to Jagdaluk, the last two miles being littered with the bodies of Indian and British soldiers, all stripped and lying where they had fallen. Lawrence managed to rescue a subedar of the 37th who he took up behind him on his horse and an old Hindu treasurer who was carried by a friendly

Afghan. At their destination they found General Elphinstone, Brigadier Shelton and Captain Johnson with Akbar. That day they had passed the body of Captain Skinner, who had been sent to parley with Akbar but had been killed on the way. Another tragedy was that the warning sent in cypher by Conolly, that Akbar intended to get hold of Elphinstone and the families, had arrived too late; and they were all now in the Sirdar's hands. When Elphinstone and his group of staff officers had gone to meet Akbar, they were greeted courteously, seated on cloths spread under trees and served tea and pilau. Also present were Akbar's father-in-law, Mohammed Shah Khan and several Ghilzai chiefs. Akbar promised that the next morning he would call a meeting of various other chiefs and arrange a safe escort for the remnants of the army. Whether or not he actually meant this or any of his other promises it is difficult to say. He could be kind and considerate on occasions, as the hostages were to learn, but duplicity came easily to him. He pleaded that he was unable to control the Ghilzais, which to some extent was probably true but throughout this period he played an ambivalent role, keeping all his options open. At any rate, now that he had poor old Elphinstone in his power he would not let him go. The chiefs refused to join him the next day, or so he said, and averred that it would be unsafe to allow the General and his party to leave.

At Jagdaluk, after they had met up with Elphinstone, Shelton and Johnson, the hostages learnt that on the morning of the 10th the remnants of the force had marched towards Tezeen being fired on but unable to return the fire because, according to Lawrence, who admittedly only had the news at second hand, 'Our military authorities, who proved themselves as incapable of conducting a retreat as they had previously shown themselves in all the operations preceding it, had with the most strange perversity, ordered our men on no account to open fire.' The ranks had been forced inwards before being slaughtered. Apparently Akbar had offered his protection if the soldiers surrendered their arms although the officers could keep their swords. This was rejected on the grounds that it would be dishonourable, on which Lawrence's caustic comment was: 'The dishonour, and it was deep and indelible, had already been incurred in commencing a retreat which was clearly avoidable, but which when once commenced, could not by scarcely any human means have turned out otherwise than utterly disastrous.' They learnt that at Jagdaluk, the very place where they were halted for the night, the remnants had sheltered behind some ruined stone walls but even there they could not escape the volleys fired from the hills. Captain Marshall of the 61st N.I. led a counter-attack of twenty British soldiers, being killed in the attempt; but at least the enemy was forced to retire.

This was when, as there were now only 150 men of the 44th, 16 dismounted horse artillerymen, 25 troopers of the 5th Light Cavalry and no sepoys left in the army, Elphinstone had had no choice but to comply with Akbar's 'request' and left with Shelton, and Johnson as interpreter. Of Akbar's proposal that each European soldier should be mounted behind one of his followers to protect them from the Ghilzais, Lawrence wrote, 'It is probable that the Sirdar was for the first time sincere in this offer, for the few survivors, less than 200, were no longer a

Jugdellah.

source of dread while their preservation might prove very useful for his ulterior motives. But with the fatal indecision that adhered to all their measures the General and Shelton demurred to this on a point of honour.' Having abandoned the treasure and lost 5,000 men, they still talked of honour and spent the night in fruitless discussion. On the other hand, perhaps they were right for in the months ahead Akbar was to show little consideration for the soldiers who trudged along with the hostages and on several occasions left them behind.

In any case it was far too late for heavy musketry fire was heard in the morning, when the troops, despairing of their senior officers' return, started moving off again. They reached a pass where they were stopped by two barricades where most of them were killed trying to force their way through. Nevertheless, 20 officers, 50 men of the 44th, 4 troopers and 300 followers managed to clear the defile at night and to reach Gandamuk where they took up a position to the left of the road, although they could only muster about twenty muskets between them. The Afghans approached, offering bread. Perhaps it was a ruse, possibly not; but certainly, when a few soldiers opened fire, their fate was sealed. Major Griffiths, Captain Soutar and Mr Blewitt were taken prisoner; the rest were massacred, apart from a small party of officers who pushed on fast, hoping to get away from their pursuers by long marches, but this was not to be and apart from a few later stragglers the only survivor to reach Jelalabad was Dr Brydon. 'Thus', wrote Lawrence, 'perished our Kabul army, sacrificed . . . to the incompetency, feebleness and want of skill and resolution of their military leaders.'

On 14 January the hostages, now also including Elphinstone and Shelton, set out in a northerly direction, escorted by Akbar and the Irregular Horse, which had gone over to him en masse. Lawrence, whose supply of tea proved invaluable, wrote, 'One poor lady, who had been confined only a few days before the army moved, declared she owed her life to its sustaining qualities. During the whole of these trying marches I felt truly proud of my countrymen and women; all bore up so nobly against hunger, cold, fatigues and other privations of no ordinary kind as to call forth the admiration even of our Afghan guards.'

They passed through a narrow valley and ascended a steep gorge before climbing a pass, from the top of which there was a view of barren mountain ranges with no signs of cultivation except by the banks of the Kabul river far below. The descent on the far side was as tedious as the ascent, made even more unpleasant by the sight of hundreds of miserable followers and sepoys, naked, wounded and frostbitten, some of whom were huddled round the remains of bushes they had set on fire for a little brief warmth. Lawrence heard a voice behind him crying out and galloped back to see a camel from which a group of Afghans were dragging some British soldiers from its kajawah. He ordered them to stop and was helped by some of Moosa Khan's men who drove off the marauders. After that he ensured that the soldiers stayed in front of him for the rest of that day's journey.

That night they were forced to bivouac in the open as the people in the fort where they halted refused to accept them, referring contemptuously to them as Kafirs. Most of them slept covered by their posteens using saddles as pillows. However, they again managed to make a shelter of boxes and luggage for the women and children and at midnight they were given pieces of boiled mutton and half-baked cakes which Akbar asked Lawrence to distribute. He professed great friendship for Lawrence and Lady MacNaghten, 'probably,' thought Lawrence, 'because we were the only individuals in the party who possessed any baggage . . .'

Despite the bitterly cold wind and the prevailing dust, even at this hour, they slept well, setting off early the next morning. They reached a ford over the Panjsheir river, dividing it into two streams, where the ladies were carried across by Afghan horsemen. Even Lawrence had to confess that 'nothing could exceed Mohammed Akbar's and Sultan Jan's anxiety until all had been safely got over, they themselves carrying two of the ladies'. This was little wonder considering the value of the ransom money they hoped to receive, or failing that, the resale possibilities of the captives in their possession. Akbar had told Lawrence to wait on the near bank until all the party were across, and whilst there he saw an old servant who had been in his employ for twenty years, vainly offering rupees to an Afghan horseman to take him across. Lawrence dashed into the stream and made the man mount behind him, getting him across only just in time before a body of plunderers attacked those still remaining on the far bank.

By this time the rest of the party were well ahead, and whilst Lawrence was riding along on his own in a leisurely way he was joined by some Kuzzilbash horsemen who were surprised at his solitary state when he could be shot at by the inhabitants of the villages he was approaching. However, nothing happened and he jogged along safely with the Kuzzilbash until rejoining the column. They crossed a wide and rapid stream in a valley studded with forts and high-walled villages whose inhabitants hurled abuse at them. Lawrence, who was at the rear of the column, came across Mrs Mainwaring who had fallen off her pony, her baby fortunately still in her arms although crying loudly. He remounted them and rode beside her until catching up with the others.

They passed a tomb which their captors told them was that of Lamech, the father of Noah, and regarded as a place of great sanctity, and by mid-afternoon they reached the large village of Teerghurree where there were a number of Hindu shopkeepers who were kind and compassionate towards the hostages' circumstances, in contrast to the Afghan women they had passed on the way, who jeered at the European females, calling them immoral scarecrows, their garments now being filthy and in rags. However, the irrepressible Eyre thought that the Afghan guards were most 'agreeable travelling companions, possessing a ready fund of easy conversation and pleasantry with a certain rough polish and artless independence of manner, which compared with the studied servility and smooth tongued address of the Hindoostanee nobles, seldom failed to impress our countrymen in their favour.'

On the 16th they held a church service, referred to by Lawrence as 'a melancholy but deeply impressive service, frequently interrupted by the tears and long-drawn sobs of some of our number'. That evening they heard shooting and were told by Akbar that he had cut off the ears of some looters and that as they were in an open, unwalled, lowland village which was not considered safe, he would have to take them higher up for greater security.

Consequently, they all assembled early the next day before being marched off under the protection of an escort of two or three hundred men armed with jezzails. Akbar, Sultan Jan and other chiefs sat on their horses beside the track watching the column, now including fourteen or fifteen sick and wounded British soldiers, pass them before closing up behind, in order to prevent the ferocious Ghilzais, who were swarming around, from attacking. A friendly Afghan told Lawrence that they had now reached a point of extreme danger and offered to take a message to General Sale. This was declined as the concensus feeling was that they must now accept their fate but that all would come right in the end. A number of Hindu clerks who had hitherto stayed with them had heard that the Europeans were doomed and stayed behind in the village with their compatriots, although Lawrence's Hindu servants chose to remain with him. It was at this low point in their fortunes that Akbar told Lawrence of the total destruction of the army and of Brydon's lone arrival at Jelalabad.

It was made worse by the knowledge that they were now only thirty miles from Jelalabad, so near and yet so far, and that their future movements would inevitably take them further away from their friends there. Lady Sale wrote: 'Thus all hopes of going to Jelalabad were annihilated; and we plainly saw that, whatever might be said, we were virtually prisoners until such time as Sale shall evacuate Jelalabad.' She and the others knew by then that Elphinstone had ordered this craven action as well as the return of the Dost from India as part of the humiliating terms to which he had agreed. Fortunately the message never got through. In the afternoon they reached Buddeeabad where there was a newly built fort belonging to Sirdar Mohammed Shah Khan: a square building with walls thirty-five feet high, a bastion at each corner and surrounded by a deep ditch. Lawrence was given the task by Akbar of distributing people to the rooms in the inner fort, occupying two sides of the square. There were a number of rooms, in the first of which were Lady MacNaghten, Mrs Boyd and her two boys, Mrs Anderson and two daughters, Mrs Eyre and her son, Mrs Mainwaring and her infant and the orphan girl, Hester Macdonald. It was separated by a wooden partition from another room housing Boyd, Anderson and Eyre, which became a mess room in daytime. A third room housed Lady Sale, Mrs Sturt, Mrs Trevor with seven children and her English servant, Mrs Smith, Mrs Weller and child, and Mrs Ryley. A fourth was occupied by Mackenzie and his Madras-Christian servant Jacob, Ryley, Weller, a clerk called Fuller and a wounded soldier of the 44th being looked after by Mackenzie. The bachelors were in a fifth room, servants and baggage were in another. Three European or Eurasian women, wives of soldiers, had an underground room. The soldiers capable of moving were in a stable close to the picket line of the hostages' horses and ponies and in a small shed were the son of Sergeant Wade who was dying of frostbite and only lasted another week, plus a soldier of the 44th who had been wounded in both legs. Elphinstone, Shelton and Johnson were 'guests' of Akbar elsewhere in the fort.

After all the accommodation had been assigned Akbar visited the ladies and asked Lawrence to explain to Lady MacNaghten that they too were his 'honoured guests' whom he would take to Jelalabad as soon as the roads were safe, and in the meantime they could write to their friends from there; Lady Sale took the opportunity to send a guarded letter to her husband. Lawrence complained of the rudeness of one of Akbar's servants who thereupon had him flogged as an example to the others, and even offered to cut off his ears, which Lawrence declined. Akbar also told Lawrence to give him a list of articles needed for the hostages' daily consumption which Moosah Khan was ordered to supply. In return for this apparent generosity Lawrence presented Akbar, at Lady MacNaghten's request, her husband's fine grey horse which Lawrence had been riding himself. At the same time he gave to Sultan Jan a gold repeater and a diamond ring which he had saved from the government durbar stores.[1]

On 18 January, Akbar, Jan and the other chiefs rode off, leaving the party in the charge of Moosah Khan, to whom Lawrence gave his handsome silver hookah, and at her request, one of Lady MacNaghten's shawls which he had coveted for some time. She and Lawrence were the only ones with any possessions and it was thought that these gifts would ease the lot of the hostages. Lawrence gave Moosah Khan a list of their daily requirements for sheep, flour, rice, ghee and wood; and his own faithful servants helped him in the daily duty of distributing supplies and killing, dressing and dividing up the sheep carcasses. For the most part they still ate with their fingers as there were only a few plates and some brass drinking vessels.

On the 19th, the day that Captain Johnson was able to change his clothes for the first time since leaving Kabul, Lady Sale wrote, 'We luxuriated in dressing, although we had no clothes but those on our back; but we enjoyed washing our faces very much, having had but one opportunity of doing so before, since we left Kabul. It was rather a painful process as the cold and glare of the sun had three times peeled my face from which the skin came off in strips.' That day also they made a coffee substitute from parched rice and barley and had 'a grand breakfast' of dahl and radishes, enjoying the change from chapattis made from coarse attah mixed with flour. 'Eating these cakes of dough is a capital recipe to obtain the heartburn.' Whilst they were at this place two sheep were killed daily for the hostages, which were cooked by Afghans, of whom Lady Sale quoted Goldsmith: 'God sends meat; but the devil sends cooks.' They also received some greasy skins and bones, boiled in the same pot as the rice, all in a lump. Few possessed any cutlery and most ate Indian fashion, with their fingers, the chapattis acting as plates as well as bread. They detested the rice which Lady Sale thought 'was rendered nauseous by having quantities of rancid ghee poured over it, such as in India we should have disdained to use for our lamps'.

A few days later she wrote, 'There are very few of us that are not covered with crawlers and although my daughter and I have as yet escaped, we are in fear and trembling.' Eyre too had been 'much pestered by vermin . . . the first discovery of a real living louse was a severe shock to our fine sense of delicacy but custom reconciles folk to anything'. On the 20th, Moosah Khan who had looked after the hostages – 'a man of low habits and indifferent character', according to Lawrence, and in Eyre's view, 'a consummate rogue even among Afghans' – left them to be replaced by an old horse dealer, Mirza Bahuddin, well known to Troup.

They were visited a few days later by a couple of chiefs who were amused to see Lawrence drilling the children, to give them something to do and get some exercise. That day also Lady Sale heard from her husband, whom she invariably referred to as 'Sale'; and Pottinger had a letter from Macgregor, the political officer in Jelalabad. The next day Akbar returned and when Lawrence mentioned the hostages' lack of money he offered to send them 1,000 rupees, but when Lawrence started to write him a receipt, Akbar tore it up, saying that such things were for traders and not necessary between gentlemen. He asked Pottinger to send a full account of the Kabul rising to Macgregor and tried to get him to insert in it orders to evacuate Jelalabad but found it difficult to believe that, as Pottinger had said, he had no power to give orders being a prisoner at the time. Akbar and the other chiefs had little understanding of British military hierarchy, regarding the political officers, mostly Captains and a few Majors who could speak Persian or Pushtu, as more important than senior officers with no linguistic skills.

By now poor old Elphinstone was in a bad way. He had been wounded in the thigh and was suffering from mental confusion as well as his other ailments. Pottinger's wound was also still not healed, although those of Troup and Lady Sale were much better.

On the 24th, their custodian, Bahuddin, brought Akbar's 1,000 rupees for Lawrence to distribute fifty to each of the officers and ladies, the rest to be shared amongst the British soldiers. There were also chintzes, long cloth, needles and thread to be shared out among 'the ladies and women'. Lady Sale wrote, in her usual acid vein, 'I fancy that he is generous at little cost: and that it is all part of the plunder of our camp.'

On this day also Conolly wrote to tell them of conditions in Kabul 'when the King [i.e. Shah Shuja] holds durbar regularly at which all the chiefs attend. He pretends to have shaken off all connection with our Government but secretly sends me messages, professing all sincerity and attachment . . . The religious feeling against us continues very strong.' The hostages in the city were under the protection of Mohammed Zeman

Khan, a Barukzye chief who never wavered in his support for them. Conolly wrote of him '. . . the Nawab's kindness is beyond description . . . He is most deeply distressed at the treacherous conduct of the chiefs . . . Mohammed Akbar is continually writing for guns and ammunition but not a man can be induced to march without pay and everyone is jealous of Akbar Khan's rising power.' Zeman Khan had even raised a force of 3,000 men mainly in order to protect the hostages and never wavered in his attitude towards the British – a fundamentally humanitarian one. Poor old Shah Shuja, on the other hand, had run with the hare and to some extent hunted with the hounds almost since his return to Kabul. Captain Macgregor, the political officer in Jelalabad, thought that he was 'more or less implicated in the insurrection'.

Three days later, whilst they were still at this same fort of Buddeeabad, Lady Sale received from her husband a chest of drawers and a quantity of clothes, which had been allowed to reach her untampered with. She also learnt that Sale had made another sortie out of Jelalabad and that Major General Pollock (later Field Marshal) had arrived at Peshawar to take command of 'The Army of Retribution'.

Akbar came back again on the 29th to ask Pottinger to alter sections in his letter to portray him in a more favourable light, bringing with him a Hindu clerk who could read English; for whose services there was to be no use. He also brought welcome supplies of boots and shoes, letters, newspapers and clothing, sent from the Jelalabad garrison, even though they themselves were beginning to run short. George Lawrence learnt that his brother Henry (later of Lucknow fame) was at Peshawar with Pollock's force advancing towards Jelalabad. He also read that three British officers had managed to get within musket shot of Jelalabad before being killed.

A few days before, Lawrence had gone for a walk with Dost Mohammed Khan, taking with them the Trevor boys, and was exhilarated to be in open country again; and after prayers on Sunday the 30th Sultan Jan invited anyone who wanted exercise to go walking with him. He went off with several children, to whom he gave lumps of sugar cane, being especially kind to little Edward Trevor, for whom he always asked. However, despite being, in Lawrence's opinion, 'a fine tempered man . . . he was also very bigoted with overweening ideas of his own prowess'.

On 10 February more boxes were received from Sale, but, according to Captain Mackenzie, Mrs Eyre was unable to get even one or two needles out of Lady Sale, although young Mrs Mainwaring, who also received a box from her husband in Jelalabad, distributed the contents among the other ladies. Perhaps this reflected the attitudes of society at home. Mrs Eyre was the wife of a mere Lieutenant whereas Florentia Sale was married to a general. She was courageous, every inch a soldier's wife of long experience, outspoken in her criticisms, refusing to see any good in her captors. She was, however, fiercely loyal to young people who had some sort of call on her, such as Lieutenant Mein of her husband's regiment. She rarely mentioned Lady MacNaghten for whom she appears to have had little respect because of the other lady's civility to her husband's murderer. She never mentioned the soldiers' wives, but then neither did the other diarists – until they kicked over the traces, like Mrs Wade later on. Did they join in the share-out of Mrs Mainwaring's goodies? We are not told.

Whilst they were still at Buddeeabad an old acquaintance of Lawrence's, Abdul Ghaffoor, arrived from Jelalabad with more letters and papers, accompanied by Major Griffith and Captain Souter, both of whom had been wounded, as well as Mr Blewitt, a civilian clerk, who had been taken prisoner at Gandamuk. Akbar was enraged to learn that both Pottinger and Lawrence had sent letters to Macgregor by a Kossid, a professional carrier, which he had intercepted. As a result all the officers' arms were taken away from them, although after remonstrances he returned those of Elphinstone and Shelton and to Lady Sale her son-in-law's sword. Even she was prepared to admit that Akbar had acted 'in the handsomest manner evincing much feeling on the occasion'.

On the 19th they had other things to think about when they experienced an earthquake, the first of a whole series. Lawrence wrote, 'I felt the ground shaking and suddenly convulsed under my feet,' and as the hostages rushed out of their rooms, large chunks of the lofty walls fell in on all sides and the whole fort seemed to rock to and fro. Lady MacNaghten's room sank several feet and Lady Sale's fell in with an awful crash. Fortunately, she and Shelton were on the flat roof at the time and had lucky escapes. Private Moore, Shelton's soldier servant, rushed up and carried him down. They all assembled in the centre of the courtyard as far as possible from the crumbling walls near a long, low building which suddenly disappeared leaving a yawning chasm. Whilst the British stood still, the Afghans called on Allah and the animals plunged about in terror, several getting loose. Lady Sale's description of this event was typical of her: she had been on the roof of the house supervising the washing of her clothes by a servant before hanging them out to dry and wrote: 'We dispense with starch and ironing and in our present situation we must learn to do everything that is useful . . . when the earthquake first commenced in the hills in the upper part of the valley, its progress was clearly defined, coming down the valley and throwing up dust like the action of exploding a mine – I hope a soldier's wife may use a soldier's simile . . .'

The next day they learnt that the nearby town of Paghree had been almost totally destroyed and that all the neighbouring forts had been damaged. Fortunately none of the hostages had been hurt but the Afghans were divided as to whether God was punishing them for treacherous conduct towards the infidels or for not killing them. There were further shocks the next week but again there were no casualties except for Lady MacNaghten's cat which had to be dug out.

A few days after the first earthquake they were joined by Captain Bygrave, paymaster to the army,[2] who, when total disintegration had set in, hid amongst the ravines, ultimately having to surrender to a Ghilzai chief who handed him over to Akbar. One of his feet was badly frostbitten. Whilst at this place they heard further information about an unsuccessful attack on Jelalabad, which Akbar had made. He had boasted that he would take it in two days, to which Lawrence had responded that he would not do so in three months, saying, 'You have not frost and snow to fight for you as at Kabul'.

One night there was another tremor whilst they were all lying out in the open. The following day, as on previous occasions, Lawrence raced the Afghan guards round the courtyard, usually beating them. He felt 'all the better for the excitement as well as bodily exercise'. The deprivation of this was keenly felt by officers accustomed to morning and evening rides every day.

On 1 March Mirza Bahuddin said he had Akbar's orders to search the boxes belonging to Lady MacNaghten and Lawrence, which had long been objects of acquisitive envy on the presumption that they contained many valuables. He took Lawrence's 'Star of Durani' order, awarded him by Shah Shuja, as well as his Ghazni medal and two of Lady MacNaghten's best shawls, which she gave him on Lawrence's advice, to keep him from searching the box himself. On this day also those Hindu servants still with the hostages, who were suffering from wounds or frostbite, were ejected from the fort, having first been robbed of their few possessions. Although Lawrence managed to get a few readmitted, they were sent out again a few days later. Then, in response to Lawrence's letter of remonstrance Akbar said he had only ordered out those who were totally incapacitated because of the cost of maintenance; and that Lawrence could keep as many as he wanted. Fortunately a number had stayed around outside the camp and were once again readmitted.

Ten days later Dost Mohammed Khan and Imamuddin Woordee, who had held a senior post under Shah Shuja, told Pottinger and Lawrence that Sale's position at Jelalabad was very strong and that some of Akbar's men were becoming disaffected with their failure to take it. They also learnt that a man who had attempted to murder Akbar had been roasted alive. This was thought to have been instigated by Shah Shuja or even by Macgregor, for whose power and influence the Afghans had great respect. It was then, only a few days later, that they were told of the murder of Shah Shuja himself, by a son of Zeman Khan, a good man who was so horrified that he had cut his son off and refused to see him. On this day their jailers were changed again. Bahuddin, who had asked for and had been given a certificate to say that he had treated the hostages well, was replaced by Nazir Saleh Mohammed Ghilzye, a tall, gaunt, savage-looking man.

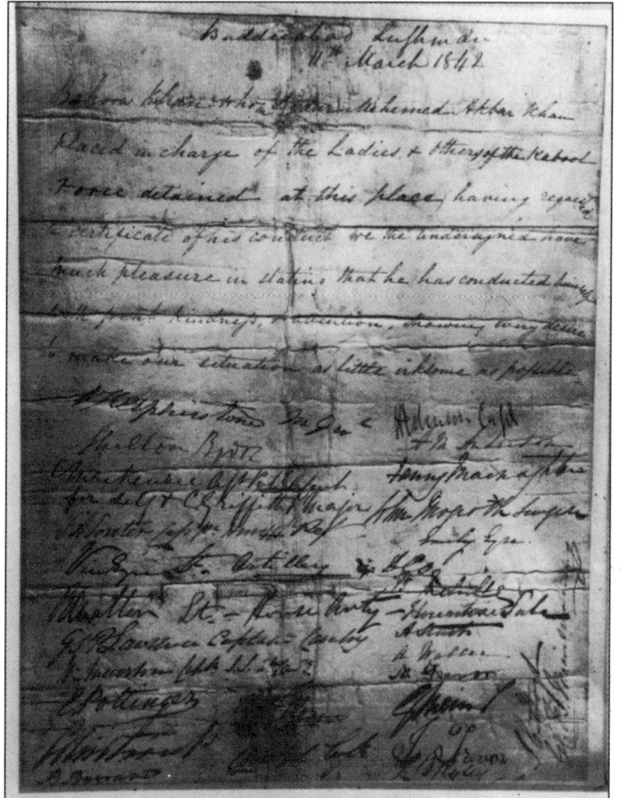

Buddiabad Lughman
11th March 1842.

Bahram Khan whom [illegible] Mahomed Akbar Khan placed in charge of the Ladies & others of the Kabool Force detained at this place having requested a certificate of his conduct we the undersigned have much pleasure in stating that he has conducted himself with great kindness & attention, showing every desire to make our situation as little irksome as possible.

Signed confirmation of Akbar Khan's fair treatment of the hostages – 11 March 1842.

On Sunday the 20th, whilst the British were holding a church service, there were several earthquake tremors but a pleasanter event was Akbar's issue of tea, sugar, chintz and long cloth, which Lawrence had to distribute. By now they had become rather more comfortable, housed in temporary matting sheds to replace the accommodation destroyed in the earthquakes. They also now had stools to sit on and charpoys for sleeping instead of having to lie on the ground.

The following day they were visited by Sultan Mohammed Khan, brother of the fort's owner, who hinted that 10 lakhs of rupees would secure their release, and was referred to the British authorities in Jelalabad. He was probably flying a kite on behalf of Akbar who never forgot the value of his charges. Meanwhile the routine of existence continued until 9 April when they heard from Mohammed Shah Khan that two days before Sale had made a successful sortie out of Jelalabad, surprising Akbar's camp, capturing his guns and nearly getting Akbar himself. A council of war had apparently been held by the chiefs after this defeat at which it was proposed that the hostages and prisoners should all be killed. Akbar, who saw his potential profit vanishing, demurred and proposed instead that they should be moved further from Jelalabad and any chance of recapture. On hearing this, Pottinger and Lawrence urged Mohammed Shah Khan to take them to Sale where terms would be agreed; but despite his earlier kite-flying he now said that he was bound to follow Akbar's fortunes wherever they led.

The next day Johnson found that his saddle had gone and men came from Mohammed Shah Khan to say that the horse was now his property. He was obviously smarting at the Afghan defeat and also ordered Lady MacNaghten to open her boxes.

After their long stay at Buddeeabad they were now to be on the move again, under stricter controls. The day after hearing this news they had packed up their goods ready to move and were told that they would have to give up their horses for yaboos, from which it would be harder to escape. They were also told that the British soldiers could not go with the hostages; on hearing this their formerly faithful servants declined to go any further with them. These even included a servant of Lawrence's who had been with him for twenty years. He had heard that the sahibs were all heading for certain death. After covering four miles the party was ordered to return as a dispute amongst the chiefs about their disposal had prompted Akbar to order their return for fear of ambush.

They finally left on 11 April, marching over a low ridge into cultivated country, crossing a river where, on the further side, they saw Akbar in a palanquin, looking pale and ill with a wounded hand in a sling. He returned a courteous salutation and beckoned Lawrence to join him. He praised the gallantry of the British attack in which General Sale had been conspicuous, mounted on a white charger at the head of his men. The hostages were housed on the far side of the river in three tents in a pleasant green place in a valley described by Lady Sale as 'beautiful under cultivation; and to us doubly so, from our not having seen a blade of grass for so long a time.' In particular, they enjoyed looking at flowers again, including several kinds of cranesbill, gentians, forget-me-nots and campions. After their long winter confinement in one place they were glad to be out in the open again although no-one knew their destination. All around there were the signs and sights of spring and Eyre, despite his situation, rejoiced in them. From now on, wherever they went he was keenly interested in the countryside around him. Like other travellers before and since, he came to realize that Afghanistan is not all jagged and barren mountain ranges but has also lush green valleys rich with cultivation as well as shrubs and wild flowers of many kinds. On one day he noted holly oak, wild almond, several species of mistletoe and a jasmine-like flower on an evergreen shrub.

Before starting off the next day they heard that the bachelors were to be separated from the ladies and the married men but when Anderson remonstrated about this Akbar relented, but then, turning to Lawrence, 'with a diabolical look', added, 'But I can tell you that as long as there is an Afghan prisoner in India or a Feringhee soldier in Afghanistan, so long will we retain you. When you can ride you shall ride, when you cannot walk you shall be dragged and when you cannot be dragged you shall have your throats cut.' At times he could be surprisingly considerate and kind but he was also known for having avenged his enemies in terrible ways and those in his power were never quite certain which side of him was the real Akbar. When he left, Mohammed Shah tried to explain that he did not really mean what he had said. They continued their march, crossed a river and found that a camp had already been pitched. They were given two old goats for their meal which the hostages returned to their captors who sent back instead two thin and elderly sheep with which they had to make do for their rations.

They set off at eight the next morning, halting at the top of a pass after a march of fourteen or fifteen miles. Lawrence had walked carrying his little god-daughter, Georgie Anderson, in his arms, having given up his pony to a young mother, much to the amusement of the Afghans, to whom such behaviour was incomprehensible. So also was it for Akbar who, seeing Lawrence on foot, sent over a couple of horses which Lawrence gave to some footsore soldiers. At the end of the day's march Akbar asked why he had done this, saying, 'A man of your rank and consequence ought not to walk on foot . . . I will fine you if you give away this horse I now make over to you.' Lawrence accepted the offer, writing in his memoirs, 'The Sirdar always took in good part whatever I said to him and treated me invariably with marked distinction, rising on every occasion of my entering and placing me on his right hand above all his chiefs.' It was again obvious that the Afghans were still unaware of British military hierarchy in which a captain was a comparatively lowly rank, but judged their captives by their political responsibilities before the campaign and their knowledge of Persian and hence many diplomatic contacts. A regimental captain would not have received such treatment.

This day, wrote Captain Johnson, 'I fell in line of march with some Afghan or other who knew me in former days in Kabul or who was in public employ under me, who was very liberal in offering to me sometimes a piece of bread, or at others some almonds and raisins; and all without exception that I came across were civil and courteous and ready to sympathise with our misfortunes.'

On the 14th the column climbed a steep and rocky ascent to the top of yet another pass. Before getting there the ladies were forced to leave their kajawahs and ride ponies, which were safer than camels under those conditions. The descent was comparatively short and they were able to rest in the long grass of a valley before covering another six miles along the left bank of the Kabul river, which they crossed on rafts made of inflated bullock hides whilst the animals crossed at a ford four miles higher up. Here they saw Akbar in a palanquin on the far bank. 'Most of us,' wrote Lawrence, 'as we landed went up and paid our respects to the Sirdar and he chatted with me for some time very affably and then gave me some pieces of bread and sugar for the children, which the Afghans always carry about with them to allay hunger on a long march.'

They were delayed the following day waiting for cattle. Then there was another stoppage as there appeared to be no camels for the kajawahs as no drivers had turned up. This could have been very serious for the ladies and weaker men, especially Elphinstone, who said he was praying for death, worn out in mind and body, and heartbroken at the destruction of his army. At last they were able to set off and halted at the fort where they had spent the night of 12 January, three months before. They found Akbar encamped with a body of horsemen and foot soldiers, and not far away a group of camp followers who had somehow managed to survive the winter.

On 16 April 'The Army of Retribution' under General Pollock forced the Khyber and joined Sale. This, together with his waning authority amongst the chiefs, prompted Akbar, after Pottinger's persuasion, at last to send an emissary to the British. He selected Mackenzie, partly because, as a 'political' he already knew him and his linguistic ability, but also because he alternated with Lawrence in taking the Sunday services and the Afghans thought he was a mullah. It was a very dangerous mission as the country was swarming with hostile Ghilzais and if he had been recognized as a Feringhee Akbar's passport would have carried little weight. He set off some days later in the charge of a well-known thief.

The new camp was in a lovely greensward and they appreciated being there for a few days before setting off again on the morning of the 19th when Akbar gave up his palanquin to Ladies MacNaghten and Sale as there were only two kajawahs with camels available. These depended on the whims of their owners and drivers whom even Akbar could not cajole beyond a certain point. The road wound up a narrow valley where the air was pestilential from the decomposed bodies of the troops still lying there. The Afghans said that many had become cannibals before death overtook them. Drenched with rain, the hostages halted for the night at Tezeen fort which had been so destroyed in the earthquakes that the ladies had to share a room already crowded with the wives of Ghilzai chiefs, awaiting departure to distant hills to avoid the expected advance of the avenging British army.

Lady Sale wrote of this day's journey on the palanquin, 'As I had to sit backwards with very little room, nothing to lean against and keep a balance against Lady MacNaghten and Mrs Boyd's baby, I benefited but little except in the grandeur of a royal equipage and my turban and habit were completely saturated.'

Akbar, who was with Elphinstone and Mohammed Shah Khan in a comfortable room with a fire, sent for Lawrence to discuss the treatment of female prisoners. In reply to some of Lawrence's complaints, Akbar responded that he had heard that one of the Afghan chiefs in India had been starved to death, which Lawrence refused to believe and the report was later proved to be wrong. Akbar, who was now clearly worried about the return of the British and wanting to capitalize on his valuable 'property', finally agreed to send Mackenzie to General Pollock to negotiate for their release. It was after this conversation that the ladies were taken over the muddy ground on the backs of Afghans to this room where they all spent the night after eating a dish of rice, sour curds and ghee, the Afghans' favourite dish, which Lady Sale pronounced to be 'uneatable'.

The next day the bachelors and the married families were separated in order to continue their journey by separate routes. This time when Lawrence protested it was Mohammed Shah Khan who went into a towering rage. 'He is the greatest enemy we have,' wrote Eyre, 'and seems at present to govern the Sirdar completely.' They were glad to know later that he had been ticked off by Akbar. How much of this was genuine and how much a cleverly prepared act, on the lines of modern interrogation methods of alternating kind and harsh inquisitors, it is difficult to say.

Most of the hostages had to spend the night in their soaking wet clothes and some of the men had to share a room with ladies, once the Ghilzais' wives had gone elsewhere. Lawrence, who had lain down with nothing over or under him, his head at Lady Sale's feet, left the room with the other men at dawn, but

Mrs Eyre.

the ladies were not able to enjoy their seclusion as there was another earthquake and they all rushed out into the open. A few hours later Mrs Waller gave birth to a baby daughter – the fourth birth in captivity. Mrs Eyre, who seems to have been a quietly serene person (and looks it in her picture), took charge of mother and child.

They were still in this fort the following night, again lying on the bare floor, including Elphinstone, who never seemed to close his eyes and was in great pain. This was the last that Lawrence ever saw of him as he, Pottinger, Mackenzie, Macgrath, the Wallers and the Eyres were ordered to stay where they were whilst the others were moved on towards Aman Koh in the hills despite Lawrence's protest at some of the ladies having to move again so soon, and his reminder to Akbar that Dost Mohammed's ladies were given every comfort on their journey to India. They were on their way at sunset, their guards expressing great anxiety about a rumour that Futtijung, son of Shah Shuja, was going to make a sudden attack on the fort with some of Macgregor's men from Jelalabad, to force the release of the prisoners. Their road lay up the bed of a stream passing the mouth of a cave crammed with the bodies of camp followers. Some said they could hear spectral voices crying out from inside the cave. They spent that night twelve miles from Tezeen where they were joined by the families of Mohammed Shah Khan and other chiefs.

On 24 April, eight days after his mission had been first agreed, Mackenzie at last set out with Akbar's proposals for General Pollock in Jelalabad. Pollock was a much respected officer of the Bengal army, who had fought against the Mahrattas and in the First Burma War. More recently he had been political resident in Lucknow. He was therefore not only an experienced Indian campaigner but was also aware of the wider political scene and unlikely to put a foot wrong in dealing with the likes of Akbar. At dusk on the 25th three horsemen in Afghan dress were seen approaching the Jelalabad sentries, obviously very tired, riding lame horses. On being challenged, the leader, whose face was scorched by the sun and his lips swollen, announced that he was Colin Mackenzie. He was a 36-year-old widower who had served in the 48th N.I. of the Madras army, had seen hand-to-hand fighting in the Coorg campaign and had been with the Navy, suppressing piracy in the Malay straits – a worthy man to speak with General Pollock. He had had a terrible journey, disguised as a minor chief from Peshawar being sent back to his land by Akbar – the story told by his companions to inquisitive tribesmen.

Akbar's proposal was that Pollock should acknowledge him as the ruler of Afghanistan, that there should be an exchange of prisoners and that the British should leave the country. Privately he had told Mackenzie that he would settle for an amnesty and a large grant of land. Pollock refused these terms but offered a £20,000 ransom for the hostages and a promise of safety for Akbar who was enraged when Mackenzie brought him this counter-proposal at Tezeen on 3 May, ordering him straight back to Jelalabad with only a few hours rest. Pollock had no time for any further concessions as he was about to advance on Kabul jointly with General Nott from Kandahar. On the 10th Mackenzie returned to Akbar once again empty-handed, without any good news for the hostages. His arduous and dangerous journeys were generally admired, especially as they were in such a hopeless cause. Major George Broadfoot in Jelalabad wrote, 'Poor Colin Mackenzie, most noble Colin . . . has been in again on his fruitless mission. Heroism like his may gild even defeats like ours . . . his coming in here and there with death staring him in his face, going back even when Akbar's conduct seemed to release him. Above all, the motives from which he did it and the spirit in which he went, raise him to something more than the word "hero" can express.' On 16 May Mackenzie rejoined the hostages at a remote village south-east of the Tezeen valley where he distributed the 200 rupees he had drawn in Jelalabad among his colleagues. Needless to say, bureaucracy saw to it that he repaid the sum to the Court of Directors in due course.

On the day that Mackenzie set off on the first of his journeys poor old Elphinstone died and Mohammed Shah Khan promised to send the body to Jelalabad. Three days later, Akbar joined the officers who had been left behind and in a long interview with Lawrence said that he wanted to come to terms with the British authorities but did not know how to set about it, professing little faith in the outcome of Mackenzie's mission, although this did not prevent him from flying into a terrible rage when Colin Mackenzie returned. Lawrence suggested that the women and children should be sent to Jelalabad, which would facilitate an immediate arrangement but Akbar admitted that he dare not do this because of the hostility of other chiefs. As in the case of more recent hostages, there were so many interested parties that release was never simple and danger ever present.

Akbar also said that he repented of his part in recent events; and perhaps he meant it as he said it, for he was a many-sided and complex personality. Perhaps it was just because by his own admission, many of the Afghans were now deserting him.

On 28 April it was learnt that Elphinstone's body had been

sent off in the care of his devoted batman, Private Miller, who was disguised as an Afghan, but had been seized on the road by Ghilzais, stripped, pelted with stones and wounded, only surviving by pretending to be a Muslim. Akbar was incensed by the news and sent off a rescue party who managed to return with Miller and the body, which was repacked in scented wormwood leaves and despatched by raft down the Kabul river to Jelalabad where the General was given a funeral with full military honours.

Meanwhile the main body of hostages, apart from the few British officers retained by Akbar, continued on their way. Lady Sale was still too weak from fever to ride and again took Mrs Boyd's place in a kajawah, having great difficulty in such a small space because of her height and literally holding the baby. On 24 April, the day that Mackenzie set off on the first of his missions, Mohammed Shah announced that he could only give his charges attah to eat. 'I suppose he keeps all the good things for the Afghan ladies,' noted Lady Sale in her usual acid style. They made themselves comparatively comfortable in their new abode by hanging up blankets for roofs and walls and busied themselves by making small thick mats of the sort used by squatting servants.

She complained that the best and largest kajawahs were kept for the Afghan ladies, 'Whilst with us many ladies unfit to ride are forced to do so and even without side or any saddles; for myself, I would rather walk than be again packed into a kajawah.'

They heard that Amanullah Khan and other chiefs had demanded that Pottinger be sent to them or that they should receive 12 lakhs of rupees in lieu. Most of the chiefs were now beginning to see the writing on the wall and either looking for financial gain in the form of hostage ransoms, resenting Akbar's monopoly, or ingratiating themselves with the approaching British. Certainly Akbar's position was increasingly uncomfortable and he now presented himself in the guise of the hostages' only protector against predators.

On 1 May and again a few weeks later, the hostages received a large bundle of letters and newspapers brought by Mackenzie from Jelalabad and Lady Sale learnt that one of her letters describing the hostages' plight had been forwarded by her husband not only to the Governor-General but also to the Court of Directors. Later on Queen Victoria expressed her interest and concern and Lady Sale came to be known and admired by the British public. Sale himself had received congratulations from the Governor-General, Lord Ellenborough, and Sir Jasper Nichols, the Commander-in-Chief.

Eyre continued to enjoy the pleasures of spring, largely untroubled by the tortuous negotiations going on between Akbar and the political officers. He had, however, had many discussions with Akbar on artillery matters and was woken one night with a message from him requesting his help in fighting against Amanulla Khan and Futtijung. Eyre replied that he was unable to comply as he was still wounded and in any case no British officer could legally take up arms under another sovereign without prior consent. He was now able to enjoy the pleasures of the countryside. Although there was still snow on the neighbouring heights there were wild almonds and yellow dog roses in the fields as well as sweet briar, white tulip and irises, and he and his companions were able to lie in the shade of a juniper tree.

On 2 May the British officers, still separated from the ladies and their husbands, attended a conference with Akbar and a number of chiefs, including Mohammed Shah Khan, at which Akbar became highly excited, saying that in defence of the Muslim religion he had killed MacNaghten and destroyed the army but now he was being attacked on all sides: by the advancing British and deserting Afghans. The following day the main party was rejoined by the Eyres and Wallers as well as Mackenzie from Jelalabad. There was also great rejoicing at the restoration of the Andersons' girl to her parents. She had been seized by Afghan horsemen on the second day of the retreat but the indefatigable Conolly, who had heard she was in the city, persuaded Nawab Zeman Khan to buy her for 400 rupees and place her in his harem. She looked plump and well, and although she could now only speak Persian and had learnt to say 'My father and mother are infidels but I am a Muslim,' she was still able to understand English.

On the 4th 200 horsemen arrived to support Akbar and the hostages learnt that Zeman Shah Khan had invited him to take the throne. He was asleep when messengers turned up but immediately set off, taking with him Pottinger and ordering Troup to follow. Lady Sale's reaction to the news of faction fighting among the Afghans was to write, 'Now is the time to strike the blow but I much dread dilly-dallying, just because a handful of us are in Akbar's power. What are our lives compared to the honour of our country...? I have no objection to the Ameer Dost Mohammed Khan being restored; only let us first show that we can conquer them and humble their treacherous chiefs in the dust...' She knew that there had been consultations between the political officers and Akbar about terms for ransom and that it had been agreed that he should be offered 5 lakhs of rupees instead of the eight he had demanded but with her usual realism, wrote, 'The general opinion is that we shall remain in captivity until all is settled.'

On the 16th, the anniversary of her wedding, Lady Sale dined with the ladies of Mohammed Shah Khan's family, an event which she described as 'an extraordinarily stupid visit'. She thought they were 'inclined to embonpoint, largely formed and coarsely featured; their dress inelegant and of the coarsest materials... like nightgowns with coins or pieces of silver tacked on all over'. Their hair hung down in small plaits and was arranged only once a week after bathing, the tresses being stiffened with gum. The women of Kabul, in particular, coloured their hands up to the wrists as well as their nails, 'which looks as though it had been plunged in blood and to our idea is very disgusting'. The dinner also displeased her, consisting of dishes filled with pilau with sour and sweet curd, served on a dirty cloth and eaten with the fingers, 'an accomplishment with which I am by no means "au fait"'.

On the 21st she received notes from Sale including the congratulations sent to him by the Governor-General and the Commander-in-Chief on the defence of Jelalabad and the successful sortie against Akbar. There was also a parcel sent by friends in Jelalabad of chintz, sugar, candy and cheese, which was distributed amongst the ladies; and turkey cloth, jean, boots and shoes for the men.

Before long they were on the move again, this time towards

Kabul, passing a number of decaying bodies, amongst which they recognized that of Major Ewart; and on 15 May, after passing through the city, they reached a fort. Here, amongst other things, Akbar said he would take them on to Kohistan if the British took Kabul. As he also offered to go to India to take his father's place, he was obviously thrashing around for ideas to get him out of his predicament.

Meanwhile, Pollock was still at Jelalabad with the 'Army of Retribution' and Nott had reached Kandahar. Both had received orders from the Governor-General to withdraw but both were prevaricating and delaying their compliance as the new orders just did not fit the situation as they saw it. The Afghans were clearly expecting the British to advance and some were hedging their bets. Back in Kabul, Akbar had kidnapped Amanullah Khan in order to extract money from him; and Lady Sale wrote,

> If Akbar procures even one lakh of ready cash he can do much mischief by raising troops even for a few weeks to annoy our forces. The celerity by which troops are raised is quite astonishing

Kabul from the Jelalabad Road.

> to us who are accustomed to see recrults drilled for a length of time. Here every man is a soldier. The only expense attending the soldier consists in his pay, which is scanty; his horse, if he have one, is his own; and every Afghan is armed completely with three or four of these knives of different sizes, from that of as long as a sword to a small dagger, pistols and a jezail, which latter predominates here. They carry much further than our own muskets; so that when our men are beyond range to hit them they pour a destroying fire on us.

Whilst Lady Sale was musing on matters military, Eyre continued to enjoy the spring sunshine, going for a long walk in the hills 'where there was a fine bracing air and a magnificent view in the direction of the Hindu Kush whose everlasting snows and jagged peaks bounded the scene'. On his return he even heard the first cuckoo. On an earlier occasion out walking, he had had the remarkable experience of meeting an Afghan trader who had in his gear a number of his own books which he instantly reclaimed. With Boyd and Waller and only one Afghan to accompany them, he climbed some hills where they were overtaken by Ghilzais who offered to escort them to Jelalabad. Realizing that this would place the others, including their own wives, in great jeopardy, apart from endangering themselves, they declined, saying that they were just out for a botanical walk. They saw some beautiful fritilleras and a kind of asphodel bearing a gigantic spandix of yellow flowers. On their return, Mohammed Rafik was told off for letting them go by Dost Mohammed Khan, of whom Eyre wrote, 'This chief is a thorough boor in his ideas and manners and is always exhibiting some mean and silly suspicion of our intentions; had it depended on him, we should all have been shut up in dark cells or narrow cages long ago.' This was the sort of treatment received by a Corporal of the 44th who was now allowed to visit his compatriots, having been kept prisoner in a fort, ill-treated and forced to become a Muslim.

On 22 May the hostages refused to march as there were no kajawahs for the ladies and, according to Lawrence, 'The Sirdar opened his eyes at this but agreed, saying good humouredly enough, "Well, you are strange Prisoners".' They might, with equal justification, have referred to him as a strange captor. They were not delayed for long and set off the next day, the ladies slung in kajawahs on mules, as no camels had turned up. They passed the upper Tezeen fort where Elphinstone had died and once again came across innumerable corpses, some of which were little altered, having been buried in snow. Others were just skeletons. At dusk they reached the part of the Khoord Kabul pass where the ladies had joined Akbar during the retreat. Late that evening, after a march of twenty-one miles, they reached another fort where there was a crowd of Afghans outside. On being asked if he had been made a Muslim, Lawrence replied, 'No, and by the blessing of God, never shall.' Thereupon one of the Afghans asked Lawrence if he would like some wine and returned half an hour later with a bottle of sherry.

They resumed their march the next morning after a hurried breakfast, crossing over a stony pass to a level plain where there was a fine pool of water shaded by large trees where they rested for a short time before ascending the bed of a mountain stream. They came to the ancient pillar of the Minar-i-Sikunder, the monument to Alexander the Great, said to have been built on his orders. It stood on a pedestal of stones and commanded a magnificent view of Kabul, the valley studded with forts and gardens and in the distance the mountains of Kohistan and the snowy peaks of the Hindu Kush. All was peaceful until a shot was fired from the Bala Hissar where Futtijung, Shuja's son, still held out against Akbar.

Alexander's column remained in view almost the whole time as well as some other Greek ruins and another pillar. Eyre wrote, 'The whole picturesque and highly cultivated valley of Kabul was spread before us like a map; the towering mountain ranges of Kohistan and the Hinddoo Khoosh (sic) clad in a pure vesture of snow bounded the horizon at a distance of nearly a hundred miles . . .' They went on climbing for another two miles on a road that was so rocky that the ladies had to dismount and walk. At the top of the pass they rested by a deliciously cold spring before covering another three miles to the Shewakee fort belonging to Ali Mohammed Khan. They were shown into cattle sheds for the ladies, which so incensed Lady Sale that Lawrence once again

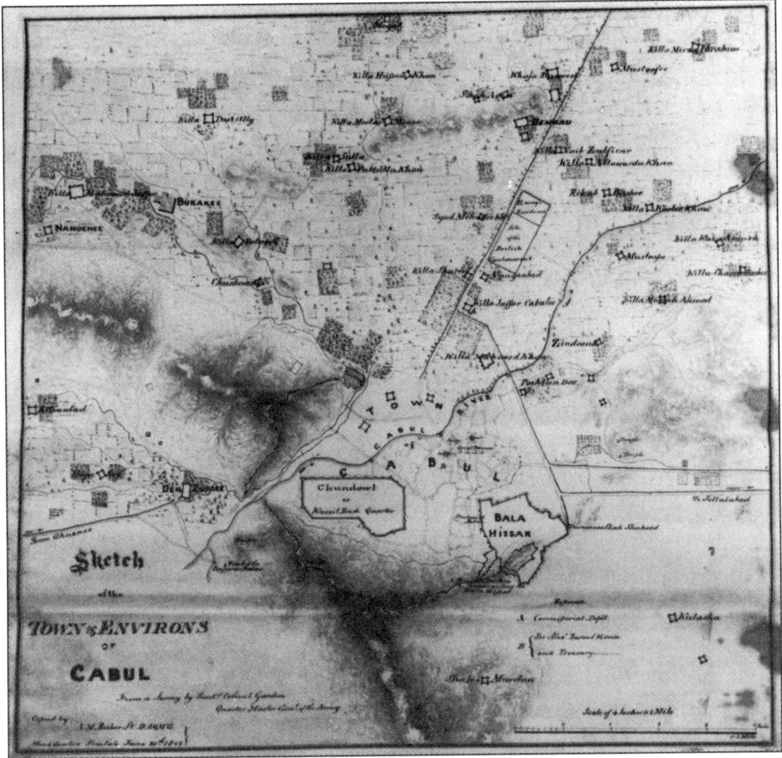

Sketch of Town and Environs of Kabul.

had to protest to Akbar who ordered the ladies of the household to vacate their quarters which were then given to the English females. These were clean, roomy and comfortable rooms, the best they had had, with access to a large garden where there was a crystal clear stream. The owner of the fort, Ali Mohammed Khan, was a Kuzzilbash, 'a polite gentlemanly man', who seemed well disposed towards the hostages despite the ejection of his family. He reminded Lawrence that the Envoy had visited this garden on one of his morning rides and quoted 'some appropriate verses of Saadi illustrating the ups and downs of human life and its great uncertainty'.

They were still at this fort a few days later when Captain Troup, who with Pottinger and Mackenzie was now lodged in the city with Akbar, visited the others and told them that the sick and wounded who had been left in Kabul before the retreat began, were all safe and well. There were also scores of Hindu sepoys and followers still crowding the streets in a half-starved condition. They had been kept alive during the winter by a little bread doled out to them now and again by Mohammed Zeman Khan and Nawab Zuba Khan. Troup returned to the city in the evening, taking with him a list of the hostages' wants for Akbar to deal with if he saw fit. Before going, he also told the other hostages about the civil war. Akbar's force was still in the outskirts of Kabul where he had been joined by Amanullah Khan; and Futtijung was still in the Bala Hissar where he hoped to be relieved by the British. Akbar wanted to wrest the citadel from him in order to get his hands on any treasure remaining but he no longer wanted to resist the British, saying that he wished that he had not been so prejudiced against them. He had had to decline Pollock's offer to release the women and children of his family because of his current difficulties. According to Eyre, quoting Troup: 'The civility of all classes to the European hostages and prisoners in and about Cabul was remarkable.'

A few days later they were paid an unwelcome visit from Suja-u-Dowlah, eldest son of Mohammed Zeman Khan, who had not forgiven him for the murder of Shah Shuja, and had turned him out of the house. He tried to persuade the hostages that he had really done them a favour but Lawrence left him in no doubt as to the heinousness of his crime.

During the next few days they learnt that the Kuzzilbash had risen against the Afghan chiefs and that Nott had won a considerable victory at Kelat-i-Ghilzye. On the 6th they heard firing and learnt that Akbar had seized Amanullah Khan, who had been the principal instigator of Burnes's murder. The behaviour of their captors began to change at this time, ensuring that they heard no further news and seizing a parcel from Jelalabad. Everything was opened by the guard on the gate who only allowed in a few items. They were unable to find out who had given these orders. However, Eyre did not allow these events to affect him unduly and wrote, 'The climate in this part of the valley we found delightfully cool and pleasant.' He saw poplar, willow and mulberry trees, a species of lupin, purple centauries in the cornfields and a delicate kind of tamarisk along the river bank.

Troup returned on 9 June, bringing the articles they had requested as well as letters and papers from Jelalabad and bottles of brandy and sherry sent by Henry Lawrence but, whilst appreciating his brother's kindness, George found that they 'had been for so long without these stimulants that few of us cared for them'. Mackenzie also came bringing them the news that Akbar had sprung a mine under the Bala Hissar but a storming party from the citadel had driven his men back. However, Futtijung had agreed to terms giving the towers to several chiefs whilst he retained the royal residence. Later they heard that Nawab Zeman Khan's sons had been taken prisoner by Akbar who was now the master of Kabul and that even the Kuzzilbash had been forced to submit.

In the meantime a letter had been received which gave the hostages hope for an early release. It was from Lieutenant Sir Richmond Shakespeare, a cousin of the author William Thackeray, who had been a political agent in a mission to Herat and to the Khanate of Khiva, where he negotiated the surrender of Russian prisoners whose detention had been largely responsible for the Russian southward advance. Shakespeare had ridden 600 miles from Herat to Khiva where he persuaded the Khan to make peace with the Russians investing the city. He then collected up 416 Russian captives and took them across the Turkestan desert to deliver them to the Russian authorities at Oranenburg, from whence he went on to Moscow to receive the thanks of the Tsar. Returning to England he was knighted in 1841 before going to India as military secretary to General Pollock in whose battles he had distinguished himself. This was the remarkable young man who was to keep his word to the hostages but not until a few more months had elapsed.

Although they noted that their guard had been increased, the hostages continued to enjoy the peace and beauty of the garden; and Lawrence continued to keep fit by running races with his captors. They learnt that Akbar had installed Futtijung as king with himself as vizier and that after his capture Nawab Zeman Khan had handed the Kabul hostages over to the chief mullah. Johnson wrote that no father could have done more, tending his own children, than Zeman Khan had done for the British and entreated that they should not be taken away.

On Sunday after their usual service, they were joined by the British soldiers who had been left behind at Buddeeabad fort. They were thin and hungry and had been badly treated. With them was a Mrs Byrne who was the wife of a soldier of the 13th of Foot who had a child with her and looked like a skeleton. She told the others of the shameful conduct of Mrs Wade, the Eurasian wife of Sergeant Wade, who had deserted him when the officers and their ladies left, in order to live with an Afghan to whom she revealed where some of the British had concealed the money that the officers had given them, including her husband's hiding place in his shoe. She also persuaded the captors to ask for more than the 12,000 rupees that Pollock had agreed to give for their release. Sergeant Wade said he would petition Pollock to have her hung but history does not relate if this was done. At the same time they also learnt that the Hindu servants left behind with the soldiers had been stripped and searched for valuables and that Mrs Wade had cruelly ill-treated the child Stoker, although Akbar had promised to send him on to Lady Sale as his father had been in her husband's regiment.

The next day they were joined by Sergeant Cleland and Gunner Dalton of the Horse Artillery; they spoke highly of their treatment at the hands of Akbar who sent a note to Lawrence to give Cleland some tea and sugar. Dalton was a mad Irishman, described by Lawrence as being 'full of fun and frolic' even in the most desperate circumstances, whom the Afghans regarded as being 'inspired', which is probably why he was spared.

Not long after, an Afghan arrived, by permission of Akbar, and produced a note from his brother Osman Khan, proposing that Pottinger, Lawrence and Conolly should meet with him. Lawrence suspected a trap and said that, as hostages, they knew nothing of General Pollock's intentions and could not take the sort of action required of them. After the man had left, Troup came again, this time with Conolly, who Lawrence had not seen since the retreat. He had remained in Kabul in charge of the hostages and the sick and wounded left in the city and had had great difficulty in raising funds for their support. In the end he had had to draw bills on India and it says something for both parties that a junior British officer could do that and the Afghans accept this mode of payment. A very high price had been set on the Anderson girl and he had been afraid of setting a precedent when he secured her release. Mohan Lal, an old friend of the British, wrote of deteriorating conditions in Kabul and that Akbar was trying to get Meer Haji to give them up to him to be taken to Turkestan. Mohan Lal himself was imprisoned and beaten; and Akbar demanded 30,000 rupees or his eyes would be put out. He wrote on the 14th to Sir Richmond Shakespeare: 'I suffer very much, sometimes I am pinioned and a heavy stone is placed on my back whilst red pepper is burnt before my nose and eyes. Sometimes I am bastinated.' Mohan Lal survived this treatment just as he had overcome other dangers in the past, when he had accompanied Burnes to Bokhara and on his first trip to Kabul. He had been used as a messenger between MacNaghten and Afghan leaders and it was his warnings just before the uprising and before the retreat that had been ignored.

Conolly brought a letter from Pollock saying that he had written to Mohammed Shah Khan to offer an exchange of prisoners 'without reserve' (including Dost Mohammed) but demanding that all captured British guns should be restored. In this letter he also stated that he now had 20,000 troops at Jelalabad and that Nott had 15,000 in Kandahar. In addition there was a reserve about to assemble at Ferozepore of 25,000, plus 10,000 British on their way from England. A few days later Mohammed Shah Khan, Sultan Jan and other chiefs arrived at the hostages' camp to ask what would be the result to themselves of such an exchange of prisoners. This, of course, was unanswerable; and after a few days' discussion an offer was made to Pollock to free the prisoners within twenty-six days if the British left the country. They must really have known that the advancing forces were an army of revenge which would not allow the fate of the prisoners to affect their advance.

On 16 July Dr Campbell visited the hostages from the Bala

Hissar, having been ordered to do so by Akbar who had heard of their various illnesses, including Lawrence with fever. Eyre thought that the fever 'probably originated in the malaria of the rice fields' as well as the stagnant water around the fort, the sedentary lives they had to lead and the poor diet on which they existed. Campbell was unable to stay long as he had many patients in Kabul, including Mackenzie and others who had gone down with typhus.

On the 24th Pottinger heard from the British authorities that he was no longer to exercise any political functions, which fortunately for the hostages, he conveniently ignored when the time came for decisive action. He learnt also that there had been little activity until the new Governor-General, Lord Ellenborough, had expressed his views about a possible alliance with the existing Afghan Government and about an exchange of prisoners. Then, just as Pollock had made his offer, he received orders for himself and Nott to press forward simultaneously, which had always been his own strategy. When the lives of so many British people who could be massacred or taken into an inaccessible hinterland had been weighed in the balance against the need for revenge and restoration of British prestige throughout Asia, it had been decided to take the risk, no doubt with Lady Sale's approval.

Akbar despatched Troup to Jelalabad to continue the parleying with Pollock, inevitably failing to bring back any favourable proposals. However, he had been able to see Henry Lawrence and returned to tell his brother George of his achievements in charge of the Sikh troops with Pollock. He had also, on his return, been able to open up a 'shop' with all the things he had bought in Jelalabad, including arrowroot, cotton gloves, reels of cotton tape, soapjelap and cream of tartar.

A few days later Akbar ordered Troup to return to Jelalabad as all his overtures were being so unsuccessful, this time taking Lawrence with him. Although advised by Dr Campbell, reinforced by Lady Sale, not to go as he was still too weak for arduous journeys, Lawrence insisted on going, first riding to Kabul to receive Akbar's instructions. Of this meeting, he wrote, 'The Sirdar received us very graciously, shaking hands with me and making me take a seat beside himself. He expressed his fear, from my pale face and weak state, that I was not strong enough for the journey, begging me in that case to give it up, adding that he could not afford to let me risk my life as I was the only person who could manage the ladies and children.' Lawrence insisted on going and Akbar gave instructions for him to get Pollock to ratify in writing the terms agreed verbally with Troup for an exchange of prisoners and the evacuation of Afghanistan by the British. Pollock, of course, had never intended any such thing and had been playing Akbar at his own game.

After visiting Conolly and the hostages in the Bala Hissar, Lawrence returned to the fort that evening before setting out with Troup at three o'clock the next morning in the company of Haji Bukhtia and a couple of noted Ghilzai freebooters, provided by Akbar for their escort. They struck across the mountain range bounding Kabul to the south-east on a road that was no more than a sheep track and almost perpendicular in places so that the horses could hardly maintain their footing. At about eleven they reached a small village where they received a friendly welcome in a shepherd's black tent. They were given some milk and a rough bed but before turning in Lawrence was able to give a couple of pills to an old man groaning with fever and to leave him a few others.

They set off again at three in the afternoon and reached the lower Tezeen fort in two hours. There were about 300 Ghilzais there who crowded round them in such an excited and suspicious manner that their escort made them move on to a higher fort, reached at sunset. The owner gave them part of his own dinner, swimming in ghee with coarse bread, apologizing for its homeliness as their arrival was unexpected. They were surprised to meet a Corporal Lewis at this place. He had become a Muslim in order to save his life and at sunset 'went through his devotions like a good Mussulman', as Lawrence put it. The two officers spread out their carpets and slept soundly until the call to prayer early the next morning.

At Lewis's request Lawrence asked the owner of the fort if the soldier could go with them to Jelalabad. The chief agreed and when Lawrence turned to Lewis and said, 'Do you desire to remain with your kind protector or go with us?' the poor man answered in his best Persian so that the chief could understand him, 'For God's sake take me with you sir.' 'Go,' said the chief' 'I did not expect this but as I have promised, you shall go.' When he heard this, 'Lewis jumped several feet from the ground in an ecstasy of joy and then bounded forward like a roe, keeping a good hundred yards in advance of us, as if afraid that the chief might recall him.'

After some miles they crossed a high mountain by such a precipitous sheep track that if their ponies had stopped at all they would have fallen on the rocks below. At nine they halted for their guides to say their prayers and when Lewis asked if he should join them and Lawrence replied that he need not do so if he did not want to, he answered, 'Then they may whistle for me,' and remained standing with the two officers. 'I wish I had known about this,' said one of the Ghilzais as he arose from his knees, 'We should soon have settled you.'

In the afternoon they reached a village where they spread their carpets under shady trees whilst their guards killed a sheep and roasted portions on their ramrods over a large fire, bringing a selection over to the British who ate voraciously. They resumed their march in the cool of the evening and at midnight reached Gandamuk, where they were so tired that they dismounted and rested still holding their horses' bridles. They were not there long and rode on until eleven the next morning, 1 August. On hearing that Major Broadfoot and a unit of sappers were out foraging a few miles away, they pushed on to meet him. They were delighted to see him and other old friends again and spent a pleasant, quiet day at his camp, sleeping on beds with sheets for the first time in eight months. Broadfoot entertained Haji Bukhtia and the guides hospitably and they were gratified by this reception. At sunrise on 2 August they left for the fourteen-mile journey to Jelalabad. Four miles out they met General Sale on his morning ride, who took them to Pollock after first alighting at Henry Lawrence's tent. Years later George wrote of this meeting, 'It is impossible to describe my feelings of intense thankfulness and delight at meeting my brother and finding myself once more among British soldiers.' For Troup this was the second time in a fortnight, but for Lawrence it was a special joy as all three brothers, who were later to work together in the Punjab, were very close. Haji Bukhtia was amazed at the brothers only shaking hands after such a separation as he had thought they would rush into each others' arms. 'Well,' he said, 'you are an extraordinary people and I cannot make you out.'

Pollock sent for Lawrence and told him that since giving a verbal agreement to Troup he had received fresh instructions ordering him to march on Kabul. In his letter, Akbar had written, 'The General must fix the day on which he would depart,' and this rather haughty expression was made by Pollock the pretext for cancelling the verbal agreement – the two officers were ordered to return to Akbar with the reply that the General would not be dictated to. Lawrence considered this to be 'a pretty kind of communication for us prisoners to take . . .'

Henry Lawrence wanted to take his brother's place as he had at that time only one child to George's four but George refused and set out to return to Kabul 'with sad foreboding'. As they rode past Gandamuk they were urged by Haji Bukhtia to go faster as the lights they could see were the matchlocks of a band of robbers. When the officers caught up with their guides, who had gone on ahead, they found them 'parleying with some 30 or 40 most ferocious looking fellows with matches alight ready for action'. Only when it was explained that they were ambassadors from the British camp with a treaty for the chiefs in Kabul, were they allowed to proceed, the robbers remaining where they were in order to fall on another party of travellers instead. Lawrence thought them to be the most 'villainous set of cut-throats' he had ever met. Reaching Tezeen fort the next day they were again treated hospitably; and the following day they reached the start of the Khoord Kabul track at nightfall. They spent the night in shepherds' tents and early on the 10th left by the mountain road for the Bala Hissar where they were told that Akbar was still asleep and were sent on to the hostages' fort, where Haji Bakhtia left them, 'hinting darkly that the result of our ambassage would arouse the displeasure of Mohammed Akbar'.

The two Ghilzais left, singing the praises of their charges after being given a few rupees each. At the fort, Troup and Lawrence learnt that Conolly had died of fever. Lawrence wrote of this remarkable young man who had played such an important role in the lives of the hostages, 'Though young in years he was remarkable for his cool judgement, moral courage and fine temper; and his intimate knowledge of the Afghans, whose esteem and affection he had won by his chivalrous bearing.'

Eyre wrote, 'But for his influence and exertions, the detachment of sick Europeans left behind at Kabul under Lieutenant Evans would long ago have starved to death or been destroyed by violence. Large sums were advanced for their support and protection by various individuals on the security of his bare word . . .' According to Eyre, Conolly and some of the other officers whose services had been used as intermediaries, had many opportunities to escape to India but had refrained from doing so, knowing what could happen to the others still in captivity. He was one of three brothers of whom one had been killed earlier in the campaign on an assault on a fort in Kohistan and the eldest, a celebrated traveller, heavily involved in the 'Great Game' of espionage in central Asia was executed by the Khan in Bokkhara, after being kept down a well for eighty days.

Lady Sale thought highly of him as she did of Skinner who she thought could have said better than anyone else what had really happened before the uprising as he had carried a number of messages, including one sent the night before Burnes's murder. He, like Trevor, knew too much and had been put to death, in her view. Even so she felt able to write of Akbar: 'I still think he will not cut our throats – not out of love to us but because the other chiefs would resent it; as having possession of us, they could at least obtain a handsome sum as our ransom.'

She wrote those words before Lawrence and Troup returned empty-handed and Akbar's reaction might well have been to cut their throats in one of his towering rages. Instead, he received them with surprising kindness, though according to Lawrence, 'It was evident from his flushed face and bright eyes that he was placing considerable restraint upon himself.' With him were Mohammed Shah Khan, Sultan Jan, Dost Mohammed Khan and other chiefs, all of whom 'looked disturbed and angry'.

'Look,' said Akbar, in Lawrence's version of events, 'these

Englishmen have returned. I never asked if they would come back.'

'But you knew we would return, Sirdar,' answered Lawrence.

'Yes, I did,' responded Akbar, 'though my chiefs assured me you would not.'

'Would you have returned?' he asked, turning to them.

'Certainly not,' they replied. 'We are not such fools.'

After this revealing exchange they all sat down and, holding out Pollock's letter, Akbar said, 'I see the General is playing with me . . . I had thought you English were men of truth; that your word, once given, was as good as law. I now see I was in error and so end all my hopes of an amicable arrangement, and now it must be war.'

At this, Mohammed Shah Khan, half drawing his knife and grinding his teeth, broke in with: 'I knew this would be the result. The Feringhees were only deceiving us. War they want; let them have it. What is the use of talking; let us destroy them all.'

By now, however, Akbar had recovered his composure and expressed his regret at Conolly's death, offering to send the body to Jelalabad, although Lawrence said that it would be better for him to be buried where he died. He also asked after Henry Lawrence but said that he would not have accepted him instead of George, although he would have been welcome as a 'visiting guest'.

Lawrence and Troup returned to their old quarters to find that Conolly had already been buried in the garden. Several other hostages were down with fever and some were critically ill. They were able to distribute letters and papers brought from Jelalabad and a number of gold mohurs they had carried round their waists. They were questioned for hours by their eager fellow captives before at last being able to sleep on their horse rugs with their sheepskin cloaks on top.

On 12 August they were joined by Captains Drummond, Webb, Walsh, Airey and Warburton, whose wife was still in hiding pursued by Akbar's minions from place to place but managing always to keep one jump ahead. They had been the first hostages to be handed over and had survived many perils and hardships in Kabul and the Bala Hissar. Four days later, Lieutenant Melville visited Akbar in the Bala Hissar and asked if it was true that they were all to be sent to Bameean. The rumour proved to be well-founded and Akbar refused to give the ladies two days' notice or to let Melville stay behind with the Andersons, both of whom were ill with fever, saying that the Feringhees, for their part, never gave their prisoners time to get ready or even tell them where they were being taken. He may have heard this from his own family and it may well have been true. He did, however, allow Dr Campbell to remain with them. Eyre wrote 'Scarce a single lady, officer, soldier or child had now escaped the disease' i.e. the fever, from which Mrs Smith, a Eurasian employed by Mrs Trevor, had recently died.

Some days earlier Pottinger had heard Mohammed Akbar say to one of his men, regarding the hostages, 'Take those dogs away'; and it was obvious that he was becoming increasingly tense. Some of them already knew from the letters received by Lady Sale that Pollock was getting ready to move on 20 August. Her own letters to her husband had been sent on by him to the Governor-General and the Commander-in-Chief and in accordance with familiar standards of journalism her motives were being queried in some sections of the press; she was even accused of being in favour of Akbar. In reality her chief desire was to see

> Akbar Mohammed Shah and Sultan Jan hors de combat; befriend those who have befriended us and let the Afghans have the Ameer Dost Mohammed Khan back if they like. He and his family are only an expense to us in India; we can restore them and make friends with him. Let us first show the Afghans that we can both conquer them and revenge the foul murder of the troops; but let us not dishonour the British name by sneaking out of the country like whipped pariah dogs . . . I have been a soldier's wife for too long to sit down tamely whilst our honour is tarnished in the sight and opinion of savages.

In Lady Sale's view Akbar had not meant to kill the Envoy but was the victim of his own passions when carried away: 'His temper when thwarted is ferocious . . . great was the credulity of those who placed confidence in him even after the letter from Conolly confirming previous warnings.' Although she considered that Mohammed Shah Khan was the worst of their enemies she was never taken in by Akbar's apparently greater consideration for the hostages: 'Akbar is a jovial smooth-tongued man: full of compliments and good fellowship . . . to our cost he did talk over our chiefs [i.e. the senior officers], pretended friendship and inability to control Ghilzais but always with a group of horsemen when massacre was taking place . . .' He claimed that his 300 mounted men were too few to keep his promise to protect the British. At the same time he boasted of having killed the Envoy. Recently he had been known to say: 'I destroyed your army; I threw away all ties of family, deserted everything for the faith of Islam; and now I am left to bear the opprobrium heaped upon me by the Feringhees whilst no-one supports me.'

Although Florentia Sale wrote: 'A woman's vengeance is said to be fearful,' and that hers was reserved for Akbar, Mohammed Shah Khan and Sultan Jan, nevertheless she had to admit that Akbar had behaved honourably towards the hostages; and although he had dragged them all over the place, he had to some extent shared the same hardships, with his own followers and their women. He always treated them courteously and called them in a now familiar phrase his 'honoured guests'.

On 23 August the hostages were joined by Colonel Palmer, Captains Barrett and Alston, and Lieutenants Harrison, Nicholson, Poett, Willies and Crawford, with Dr Thompson, who had been taken prisoner after their surrender of Ghazni on 6 March. They had suffered much hardship and bad treatment but, although lean and hungry-looking, were in good health. Their captor had been Akbar's brother, Shamshudin Khan, who had refused at first to hand them over to Akbar. Only when he set out to oppose Nott's advance did his brother decide to do so. Each party of hostages had received news of the others' treatment but undoubtedly the Ghazni officers had had the worst of it, closely shut up in a small room without air or any opportunity for exercise. Colonel Palmer had been tortured to say where the treasure was buried. The British garrison had held out for some weeks, until their water supply was exhausted, before agreeing to surrender. They then marched out to the area of the city allotted to them where the soldiers were separated from the officers, those refusing to lay down their arms being killed. So also were Lieutenant Lumsden and his wife as well as the rest of the rearguard who had remained in the citadel for what was to have been a short period.

Meanwhile, they had to prepare yet again for another move, much to the chagrin of the ladies who had only once been given a room to themselves, much appreciated by Lady Sale, who wrote, 'After so long enduring the misery of having gentlemen night and day associated with us, we have found this a great relief.' The only males in the room were Mrs Mainwaring's baby and the Boyds' two little boys, whose father slept on the landing outside. Another improvement was that they were now able to cook their own meals, which had previously been much too greasy for their tastes. They were now given their rations direct, consisting of meat, rice, attah, ghee, oil and, more recently, fruit. They still had problems over personal hygiene, however, and had only recently managed to rid themselves of lice, referred to by Lady Sale as the infantry, the fleas being the cavalry. They also suffered from mosquitoes, flies and various other bugs.

Before they all set out once again on the move, they learnt from Akbar that General Nott had evacuated Kandahar after destroying all the guns, stores, ammunition and grain not wanted on the march, having given out that he was going to India by the Goolaree pass. Akbar, who had only partly been taken in by this deception, was not sure if this was true or if he was really making for Kabul. Lawrence and Melville tried to assure him that they had no idea of Nott's plans. Akbar could not understand why the fortifications of Khelat-i-Ghilzye and the stores should have been destroyed, not realizing that this was all a necessary part of Nott's dissimulation. 'You are an incomprehensible people,' he said, 'There is no understanding you or your intentions.'

On the 25th a herd of cattle and camel litters arrived for all except Dr Campbell, the Andersons, Mrs Trevor and their children as well as Troup and Bygrave who had suddenly received orders to remain, to whom the others bade a gloomy farewell at 10.30 that night as the convoy set out in bright moonlight, some walking, others on horseback or camel litters, escorted by 300 or 400 men under the command of Saleh Mohammed Khan, formerly a subedar in the Afghan levies who had deserted with all his men. When Lawrence addressed him as Subedar, he said he was now a general. Leading the march were 'half a dozen Hindustanees playing bugles, fifes and drums'. 'At another time,' wrote Eyre, 'we might have indulged in merriment at their expense; but now we were too sick in heart and frame to indulge our sense of the ludicrous.' Lawrence was also oppressed by the thought of the uncertain future now that negotiations for their release had broken down and they were going further away from their compatriots. It was the most mournful of their many moves and some were very despondent. Lawrence wrote, 'As I wended my way in the darkness, thoughts of home and all my treasures there crowded upon my mind, filling me with sadness. But there came the consoling reflection that they were safe in their native country and among loving relatives who would well supply my place if it was God's will . . .'

They marched all night, avoiding Kabul, going through gardens and orchards, and halted at 7 the next morning after covering sixteen miles, mostly on narrow roads overhung by mulberry trees, which had brushed against the camel riders to such an extent that Mrs Mainwaring had had a lot of skin rubbed off her arm. By now most of the ladies had adopted Afghan dress, including the white bourka through whose veil of white muslin and narrow eye opening they could see without being seen. Hitherto many had continued to wear their own dresses but now they were going to unknown regions they wanted to attract as little attention as possible.

At their halting place on the Ghazni road they saw Sultan Jan's horsemen on their way to fight Nott's troops. Towards evening they were joined by Dr Berwick and fifty-seven sick soldiers who had been left behind in Kabul when the army retreated and they resumed their march the next afternoon, Lady MacNaghten leading in a kajawah, followed by the other ladies and children, two to each camel, and the officers and soldiers riding or walking. In the van and rear of this now substantial column were Afghan horsemen and foot soldiers under Saleh Mohammed and Ahmed, Akbar's master of horse, who had probably been sent to spy on the loyalty of the former subedar. The infantry contingent of the escort consisted of 300 deserters from Hopkins' regiment armed with British muskets, who made great display of their discipline, mounting guard, planting sentries, playing reveille and beating retreat. Lawrence called them 'a good-humoured set of fellows' who 'laughed and chatted with us as we marched along'. Their commander, Saleh Mohammed, had dressed himself up for the march in a blue frocked coat, was mounted on a large white horse with flowing main and tail and generally gave himself great airs. Nevertheless he was to prove the means of their salvation.

After nine hours on the march they halted at a place where three small carts were added to the convoy for the ladies. They saw many camels and asses loaded with assafoetida destined for Turkestan, whose drivers gazed with amazement at this curious mixture of people. As their route led them towards Ghazni, Pottinger, Johnson and Lawrence tried to persuade Saleh Mohammed to make short marches, to enable Nott's force to catch up with them, promising him a sum of money to be contributed by all the hostages and prisoners. On this occasion he affected to be angry and refused to listen, but the seed had been sown.

On the 27th they climbed over a pass and descended into a small and beautiful valley bounded by bare and rugged mountains. Eyre was impressed by the beauty of the poplars and willows bordering a crystal clear stream, with green and yellow fields of cultivation beyond. 'Here,' he wrote, 'as we reclined our weary limbs and looked around the smiling scene which everywhere charmed the eye, we wondered that the inhabitants of so favoured a spot should be so sensible of the blessings of peace, in a land where the people are so distracted by blood feuds that they hardly dared leave their own dwellings.'

Continuing their march the next day, they met donkeys laden with goods for the Kabul market and were able to buy grapes, apples, apricots and peas. On the 28th they went on through a cultivated valley and passed a fort and walled town that Lawrence remembered from the time when he had been pursuing Dost Mohammed Khan. On the 29th they continued under the walls of a large fort belonging to Mustapha Khan, a Kuzzilbash who, in Lawrence's words, 'had the courage and humanity, in spite of Saleh Mohammed's threats to report him to Akbar, to come out and salute us, bringing us bread and fruit, at the same time sympathizing much with us and comforting us, saying "Keep up your spirits; all will go well with you."' and telling them that the country to which they were going had many Shias where the Kuzzilbash Shias had some influence.

The next day, the 30th, they were heartened by the news that the British had retaken Ghazni. They began the ascent of the Oonai pass and could see Koh-Baba, a snow-covered mountain. Once over the pass they descended to a river bed. Eyre described the twelve miles they had covered as 'very tedious' but enjoyed the abundance of a beautiful species of salvia. The next day they passed a fort whose walls were crowded with well-armed men where Saleh, fearing an attack, closed up the column and ordered his men to fix bayonets and to march with drums beating and colours flying, but there was no attack. At daybreak the following day they began the two-mile ascent of Mt Kaloo. As the road was unsafe for the heavily loaded camels the ladies and the sick had to transfer to ponies and some of the sick soldiers had to walk. Despite these problems Vincent Eyre was moved by the beauty of the scene: 'The view to the north presented a boundless chaos of barren mountain, probably unequalled in wild, terrific grandeur.' On this very tiring journey of ascents and descents they crossed a pass at 12,500 feet before reaching a fort at Kaloo. They crossed another pass at daybreak and pitched their tents within sight of Bameean, near the ruins of a fort and town, not far from the caves and colossal Buddhist figures for which the place was famous. These huge male and female figures were covered with clever representations of drapery and there were openings at the head and feet of each connected by galleries and stairs cut into the rock. Eyre thought they 'formed a wonderful scene and carries the fancy back thousands of years to a date at which a widely different race peopled the country from now existing . . . A few of the caves were inhabited by the lower orders.' The guards fired their muskets as the statues were passed, cursing them as idols. They also had a noisy row with the local villagers, which put Saleh into a bad temper not improved by the hostages, led by Lawrence, refusing to sleep in empty cowsheds. In the end he permitted them to pitch their tents instead.

On 5 September Eyre obtained permission to visit the caves and images, accompanied by a guard. He found that they were of very hard clay studded with round pebbles and that there had been some attempt to mend the mutilated sections. He ascended to the top of the female image by a series of stairs and galleries. Sitting on top of the lady's crown he was joined by a number of local people who said that they all supported the British. The next day he returned, this time with the indefatigable Lady Sale. During the days of long and tiring marches they had learnt not only about the retaking of Ghazni but also that Akbar had been defeated at Tezeen, but neither of these British victories in themselves made the fate of the hostages any more foreseeable given the uncertainties of Akbar's temper. Lady Sale heard that a subscription list had been got up by some civilians for the presentation of a sword to her husband who, from being initially criticized for not obeying orders to march on Kabul when it was patently impossible, was now regarded as a hero for his aggressive defence of Jelalabad. She was not pleased to read extracts from the English language press in India, as cavalier with truth as modern tabloids, in which she was now portrayed as a heroine leading the troops into battle (although she would gladly have done so given half a chance).

She had at first been critical of Pottinger, whose role in the surrender negotiations had been against his will, but had since come to appreciate his knowledge of Persian and of the Afghans, which was now to stand them all in good stead. Things were changing rapidly for they had been joined by a number of Afghan chiefs anxious to be on the right side of the British and Saleh Mohammed was thinking seriously of changing sides again.

On 11 September Pottinger told Lawrence that Saleh Mohammed had had orders from Akbar to take the hostages to Khooloo if the Afghans were defeated by the British advancing on Kabul. They learnt also that although the Governor of Bameean had demanded their release this was not going to happen and that the crisis they had long dreaded was now upon them, if indeed they had to march away from this friendly Kuzzilbash area. Eyre wrote 'All hope of deliverance seemed now at an end and we endeavoured calmly to resign ourselves to a fate that seemed inevitable.' On the other hand they also heard that Munshi Mohan Lal was raising a large sum of money to pay for their release and that the Kuzzilbash chiefs had threatened revenge if the hostages came to any harm.

Although Saleh had professed to have no interest in listening to ransom offers, he now changed his mind and wanted to talk. Accordingly, a meeting was held between him and Pottinger, Mackenzie, Johnson, Webb and Lawrence, attended also by an agent of the Kuzzibash chief, Shah Mohammed Reza. It was agreed that Saleh Mohammed should be given 1,000 rupees a month and 20,000 to be paid on their arrival in Kabul as well as command of a regiment in the Company's service. For comparatively junior officers they were taking a lot on themselves, especially as Saleh had once before shown himself capable of treachery, and they all knew the traditional parsimony of the Company's bureaucracy when asked to pay up. On the other hand they knew also that it was an old established custom of Indian warfare for commanders to take whole regiments over to the other side, and for the soldiers to feel only a personal loyalty to their commanders, especially in irregular units. They decided to risk it as they realized how desperate things were beginning to look with Akbar reported as saying that he would sell the whole party to the Turkomans if he was thwarted, where they would have joined the hundreds of Russian slaves already there. All the other officers signed, except the two most senior. Shelton said that the action was premature and Palmer thought it would do more harm than good. All the ladies signed and all agreed that they would make up the sum if the Government declined to pay. Saleh then showed them an order to take the hostages to Khooloo where the ruler would sell them as slaves in Bokhara. Having now decided to throw in his lot with the British again, Saleh Mohammed decided on instant action, hoisted a flag of independence (whatever that was) on the fort and drove off Akbar's Master of Horse and his followers.

On 16 September they turned round, setting off in the opposite direction, towards the British forces, leaving Bameean behind and heading for the fort at Topchee Bashee en route for Kabul. Wanting to augment the firepower of the escort, Saleh offered muskets to the British soldiers but most of the men of the 44th were now so apathetic after their privations that they refused, although the horse artillerymen accepted the offer. Lady Sale tried to shame the infantrymen by saying that she would shoulder a musket but to no avail. She thought it was 'sad to think the men were so lost to all right feeling'. They had suffered too much and had lacked even the comparative comfort enjoyed by the officers and ladies; and there were none of their own officers to spur them on. Lady Sale also paid Lawrence the great compliment of giving him Sturt's sword, saying that she knew it would be well used.

They were aroused at midnight in their new quarters by the arrival of a note from Lieutenant Sir Richmond Shakespeare who was on his way to them at the head of 600 Kuzzilbash horsemen. Lawrence wrote, 'Our joy and thankfulness at the receipt of this intelligence are not to be described and little sleep did any of us have for the rest of that night.' Only a few days before they had faced the prospect of being sold as slaves in the market at Bokhara and now deliverance was almost at hand.

They left at daybreak the next morning and reached a fort at midday. They were seated on the shady side of the fort when a cloud of dust was seen approaching. This turned out to be Shakespeare and his horsemen, who were received by Saleh and his troops drawn up in line. 'Oh, what a joyful moment was that when I saw my old friend Shakespeare and felt we were really delivered,' wrote Lawrence, who presented Saleh to Shakespeare and told him of his services. Shakespeare was given a great welcome by all his compatriots except Shelton who was offended that he had not first reported to him. When they resumed their march there was much animated renewal of old friendships with some of the Kuzzilbash soldiers, but they were still not yet out of danger and they set off again at three the next morning as there were rumours that Akbar and Sultan Jan intended to intercept them. They kept up a rapid pace until once again they halted at the fort belonging to Mustapha Khan, the Kuzzilbash, who reminded them, as his servants gave them cakes, milk and curds, that he had told them they would be freed. Although they had covered thirty miles of forced marching that day they – or at least some of them – were still able to appreciate the scenic beauties of their route, stopping on one occasion, according to Eyre, 'by the side of one of those small gushing rivulets, the gladdening murmur of whose crystal waters so constantly greets the traveller's ear throughout Afghanistan'. They appreciated also the Kuzzilbash hospitality, especially the kindness of the old chief who had spread carpets in the shade of poplars and arranged for them to be served with tea in china cups, European fashion. As Mackenzie was taken ill at this place he and Eyre stayed there after the others had left and in the evening when Mackenzie felt better, the chief escorted him and Eyre, who had remained with him, on their way, pawning a snuff box in order to buy them a present of fish.

On their way again at dawn the next day, they were delighted to meet shortly afterward a British officer who told them that Sale's brigade was advancing towards them. After a few more miles they met up with General Sale himself, with Henry Lawrence and other officers. Later they came up with the 3rd Dragoons, the 1st Light Cavalry and before long also the mountain train, HM's 13th Light Infantry and Broadfoot's sappers. They moved on together towards the heights which were crowded with British bayonets, where the 13th Light Infantry gave three cheers for each of the ladies and the mountain gunners gave a royal salute. 'That evening,' wrote Eyre, with masterly understatement, 'we found ourselves in circumstances far more favourable than we had known for nine tedious months of suffering and sorrow.'

Lawrence took care to present Saleh to Sale, for without his second apostasy the hostages would probably not have survived. It was just as well that he did so as some of Broadfoot's men had already seized several of Saleh's soldiers, accusing them of having stolen their British muskets; and it was with some difficulty that Broadfoot was persuaded to release them.

The next day the whole force marched through the great

bazaar of Kabul where all the shops were shut and no Afghans were to be seen.

Florentia Sale, so long the stiff-upper-lipped General's wife, allowed herself the privilege of unwonted emotion, writing: 'to my daughter and myself, happiness so long delayed as to be almost unexpected was actually painful . . . I could scarcely speak to thank the soldiers for their sympathy. . .' General Sale was equally overcome by this family reunion.

They passed General Nott's camp (for the three British columns had converged on Kabul) and at sunset, met by a salute of artillery, they entered General Pollock's camp where they were surrounded by old friends wanting to greet them. One of these, a Captain Smith, wrote: 'How eagerly we crowded to see them pass along; what grasping of their hands; what hearty congratulations. The ladies were conveyed in litters, the curtains of which concealed them so that we could not observe what effect on their looks had been produced by the sufferings and hardships they had undergone.' The men were bearded and in Afghan dress, except for Shelton who had never worn it and was still in the uniform in which he had been captured. They also met their fellow captives who had been left behind and had been liberated after Akbar's defeat by Jan Fishan Khan, whose loyalty to the British had, in Eyre's words, 'rendered him houseless, childless and penniless'. Captain Bygrave, who had been forced to go with Akbar, arrived in camp on the 27th, accompanied by their friendly jailer, Mohammed Rufik. Bygrave said that he had been well treated by Akbar, who professed himself to be relieved at the hostages' safety – and he probably was too in an obscure way. Eyre wrote that his 'clemency was not altogether devoid of grace when it is remembered that clemency to an unbelieving foe is neither a principle of the Mohammedan creed nor a characteristic of the Afghan people'. He regretted that 'A man so highly endowed with talents and qualities should have perpetrated such enormities'.

Now that their captivity was over, the hostages and prisoners found time to thank those who had helped them and a letter of appreciation was sent to Sir Richmond Shakespeare signed by the ladies and officers, some of whom had been held in Kabul until the last weeks, including Warburton, shortly to be reunited with his Afghan wife. Altogether, 32 officers, 12 ladies, including Mrs Wade, 21 children, 38 British soldiers of the 44th, 7 of HM's Light Infantry and 6 of the Bengal Horse Artillery were released from captivity (the numbers vary in different accounts but these seem to be the most accurate). So ended a period that none of them was likely to forget.

CHAPTER V

The Aftermath

The disastrous retreat, the taking of hostages and the ferocious nature of the British revenge all left their scars; and the Indian armies were never quite the same again. The regiments that took part in the campaign were amongst the first to rebel fifteen years later; and enemies of the British among the rulers of the Indian states, and amongst the Sikhs and Burmans, had been made aware that the British were not invincible. The British, for their part, showed a ferocity in subsequent campaigns, determined to avenge the stains on their honour, that had been lacking before. The whole episode determined many in London and Calcutta (then still the centre of government in India) never again to become embroiled in Afghanistan; yet thirty-three years later they did just that. There was continuous argument between officers and politicians who favoured a 'forward' policy and those who did not, compounded by the changes of policy favoured by alternating Conservative and Liberal governments in London, which, after 1858 became directly concerned with Indian affairs.

This is, however, neither a military nor political book and is more concerned with the fate of individuals.

In accordance with army regulations, the statutory courts martial were held on the officers who had 'voluntarily' become hostages, including Palmer, Mackenzie, Troup, Waller and Eyre (who had been mentioned in despatches by Elphinstone) and were all honourably acquitted. Shelton was also court-martialled and, surprisingly, also acquitted.

The Sales were lionized in Britain, apparently because the authorities had decided to turn them and the Jelalabad garrison into the heroes of the war, quietly forgetting Sale's disobedience of orders. At the end of their triumphal visit to England, they returned to India at the end of 1844 and a year later General Sale was mortally wounded at the battle of Moodki. He had had half a century of campaigning in India and elsewhere, always in the British service, starting in HM's 12th of Foot in the war against Tippu Sultan in 1798 and was at the siege of Seringapatam and other operations under Wellesley. A year after his marriage in Travancore he was at the storming of Mauritius and the surrender of the island by the French in 1810. He had commanded the 13th of Foot in the First Burma War and was wounded during the advance to Rangoon, being twice mentioned in despatches; he later commanded a brigade in Burma before taking up another brigade command in Afghanistan where, with the local rank of Major General he had led the expedition to Kohistan and the storming of Ghazni, after which he had been made KCB. Florentia Sale was given a special pension of £500 a year by the Queen and settled on a small estate near the hill station of Simla. She died in 1853 in Cape Town where she had gone for her health. Under a granite obelisk over the spot where she is buried an inscription reads: 'Underneath this stone reposes all that could die of Lady Sale.' A fitting epitaph for such an indomitable woman. Her daughter, Mrs Sturt, married again to a Major Holmes and both were beheaded by mutineers in July 1857 as they sat in their carriage.

Shelton relinquished his temporary rank of Brigadier and returned to the command of his old regiment, the 44th, which he had to re-raise as so few men were left. On 10 May 1845 he fell off his horse and died three days later.

Pollock became a much respected Field Marshal but poor Nott, who became Resident in Oudh went home in 1845 and died of an illness. He was a strange man with something of a chip on his shoulder. Coming from a poor and modest background with little education, he had entered the Bengal service from the Volunteers at the end of the eighteenth century, starting his career as an Ensign in the Bengal Europeans (later called the Bengal Fusiliers) and had served against the tribes on the west coast of Sumatra. At the start of the Afghan War he was commanding the 32nd N.I. Soon afterwards he was appointed Major General but the death of his wife affected his mental health and he appeared at times to be sour and cantankerous, and not particularly interested in securing the release of the hostages.

Pottinger, the 'Hero of Herat', as the English press had called him, was another who only survived a short period of freedom, dying in Hong Kong in 1843, on a visit to his uncle.

Shakespeare, who had achieved so much as a young man, did not go on to further honours, serving in various political and military capacities in Gwalior and the Punjab. Eyre, who took a distinguished part in the relief of Arrah during the mutiny and was later at the relief of Lucknow, was knighted and retired as Major General Sir Vincent. His first wife died in Calcutta in 1851 and he married twice again.

Lawrence, not long after his release, found himself working with his brothers John and Henry, as an assistant political officer in the Punjab and was for a time a prisoner again, this time of Chutter Singh, when the Sikh troops were in revolt. Later he was with Napier at the forcing of the Kohat pass and as a Brigadier during the mutiny helped to ensure that Rajputana remained an area of comparative quiet. Ultimately he retired as Lieutenant General Sir George Lawrence.

Mackenzie went as political officer to the punitive column in various parts of Afghanistan before resuming his military career proper, commanding the 4th Sikhs and later, when commanding a division, being wounded in a confrontation with native troops during an incipient mutiny. For some reason, never explained, he received rather shabby treatment, not even getting the Kabul medal to which he was entitled, until 1853. Although he became a Lieutenant General he was never knighted. The authorities in India and Britain chose to honour, first, the Sales, and the Jelalabad garrison, then the relieving forces and only lastly those officers who had volunteered to be hostages, with the exception of Lawrence and Eyre.

Lieutenant Trower, like other young officers, was very cynical on the subject of honours. He had seen the writing of general officers' despatches entrusted to junior officers who wrote of achievements such as the taking of a fort – with great gallantry – when the subject of the despatch had not even been there. An advance as being in three columns 'in admirable precision order', Trower knew to have been 'a rush of a rabble'. He wrote of the generals scathingly as 'the sort of men to whom our army is entrusted' and stated that he could recapitulate 'all the thousand disgraceful facts connected with this campaign' but did not want to.

Alas, there is no record of the fate of the soldiers of the 44th and the artillerymen who shared their captivity with the hostages. The most remarkable survivor was Dr Bryden, the lone member of Elphinstone's force, who made it to Jelalabad and fifteen years later survived the siege of Lucknow. There is a natural tendency, after traumatic experiences, to think that later life will be happy ever after. Unfortunately fate is never so kind, but whatever vicissitudes life brings, most survivors of war are able to judge later trials by the yardstick of experience. Of the hostages, some, such as Lawrence, achieved an old age loaded with honours; others, including Shelton, Sale and Pollock lasted only a few years. Life is indeed a lottery.

Of the Afghans, the great survivor was Dost Mohammed Kahn. Restored to his throne after years of comfortable captivity in India, he went on to rule wisely for many more years, to be a staunch ally of the British and to reject Sikh overtures to join in their war of 1845 against the British, much to the disgust of his son, Mohammed Akbar Khan who continued to plot against his father and organized a Ghilzai rebellion. He died in suspicious circumstances and may well have been murdered by one of his many political enemies. His misdeeds were forgotten, his bravery and other qualities remembered and, at any rate until recently, he remained one of the great heroes of the Afghan pantheon.

Lawrence and Eyre might have regretted his passing for both admired his qualities but not so Lady Sale who rarely had a good word to say of him and even less so another redoubtable female, the Begum Shah Jehan.

For nine whole months she was on the run throughout the city of Kabul pursued by the implacable minions of Akbar. In the end she made her escape disguised as a British officer, with her two sons, leaving her older children by her first husband behind. Her eldest son, Jahan Dad Khan who was born in 1840 had his name changed to John Paul Warburton and the youngest, Robert, was born on 11 July 1842 whilst she was still in hiding somewhere in the warren of houses in Kabul. On 20 September she rejoined her husband at a Ghilzai fort on the way south to the frontier. Some years afterwards Warburton went off on two years leave to Ireland with the youngest boy but never told his family of his marriage. It is not clear how he explained the boy, who went on to English schools and Woolwich, later becoming the famous Sir Robert Warburton of the frontier where he spent more time than any other political officer. The elder boy, John Paul, who was never accepted as his own by Warburton, stayed in India and went to school in Agra, ultimately becoming one of the most famous policemen of the Punjab, where he was known as 'Button Sahib', the name 'Warburton' being too much of a handful to say. It was said that he could tell a criminal by just gazing at the faces in a crowd.

His mother, the Begum, remained with her husband during the rest of his Indian career in garrisons at Sipri and Amritsar. He also took part in the Gwalior campaign and became Lieutenant

Controller of Devils the Begum with her hookah and servants.

Colonel, commanding the Peshawar brigade, much against his will as he never wanted to go anywhere near Afghanistan again. There he died leaving a wife who had faithfully followed him, although to the end he never acknowledged her or the eldest boy to his family in Ireland. As he had never joined the Indian Pensions Fund his son Robert, then a subaltern in the Bengal Artillery, attempted to provide for her out of the capital his father had left, investing it all in a local bank which later suspended all payments. 'Button Sahib' then took the poor lady into his household in Ludhiana, a town well known to the Afghan hostages who had been held there and where she felt quite at home with the many other Afghans still there. At one time they included the family of Shah Shuja, including his old blind brother who had asked to return to India with Pollock's troops, in the charge of George Lawrence. Years later Robert Warburton junior met the family, still at Ludhiana. They were very kind to him and he was particularly impressed by the dignified resignation to their exile by Shuja's two sons, Shahpur and Nadir and their consideration for others, writing, 'I have seldom seen truer types of true gentlemen than those two brothers.' The elder was in receipt of a pension of 500 rupees and the younger of 100 rupees a month from the Indian Government – small sums indeed with which to bring up their families and support the number of ancient servitors who had been driven out of house and home at Kabul and had followed the fortunes of this royal family into the heat and plains of India.

John Paul's household became a rambling extended household with his own family and their own offspring; and was also physically vast, covering a large compound. There the Begum kept purdah in her own quarters and never allowed anyone to forget that she was of royal blood. She had retained her Afghan servants who looked after her in a state bordering on loyal slavery; and although any maid guilty of poor work was branded, they remained devoted to her. When her daughter-in-law, Mary, went to visit her in her quarters she would be kept standing the whole time. On one occasion she asked Mary to bring her some mulberries, which she then sent back on the grounds that she expected several baskets so that her servants could share them.

She smoked a hookah and remained always an Afghan lady of high rank, dying in comfort in the presence of her Afghan servants and her Afghan son. She was the most remarkable of all those who suffered deprivations after the retreat of the British.

Notes

Chapter 2

1. 'Native' was not then used in a pejorative sense. The Company's forces comprised both 'Native' and 'European' regiments. There were also regiments from Britain known as HM's, followed by a number (i.e. HM's 44th of Foot). County affiliations came later.
2. Hereafter referred to as the G.O.I.
3. Only twenty-four years before this, the Gurkhas had been fighting against the British in the third Anglo-Nepalese war of 1816.
4. The funds required for pay and for feeding men and animals was known as the 'Treasure', housed in a Treasury when a force was not on the move.
5. Jezzails were long-barrelled home-made muskets whose owners were known as 'Jezzailchees'.

Chapter 3

1. Kafirs (normally spelt with one 'f', unlike the South African term) are a mountain people, now inhabiting an area of Pakistan, who are still pagans. The word came to be applied by Muslims to all non-believers.
2. An Ayah was a female servant or nurse. To this day many European families in India employ ayahs.
3. Bhoosa was presumably some form of cereal (the author confesses to ignorance).

Chapter 4

1. Durbar stores were provided as gifts for presentation to chiefs and others at official Durbars, i.e. ceremonial meetings.
2. Johnson had been paymaster to the Shah's forces only.

Bibliography

Anon. Manuscript volume of a diary of an Officer with Shah Shuja's contingent. London 1847.

Broadfoot, W., *The Career of Major George Broadfoot*, London, 1888.

Bruce, George, *Retreat from Kabul*, London, 1867.

Collister, Peter, *Hellfire Jack V.C.*, London, 1989.

Dupree, Louis, *The First Afghan War and The British Retreat 1842: The Functions of History and Folklore*, Rome, 1976.

Eyre, Lieutenant Vincent, *Military Operations at Kabul*, London, 1843.

Fletcher, Arnold, *Afghanistan Highway of Conquest*, New York, 1965.

Hopkirk, Peter, *The Great Game*, London, 1990.

Kaye, J.W., *History of the War in Afghanistan*, London, 1851.

Kaye, J.W., *The Lives of Indian Officers*, London, 1889.

Lawrence, George, *Forty Years Service in India*, W. Edwards (ed.), London, 1875.

Lawrence, John, *Lawrence of Lucknow*, London, 1990.

Lowe, Charles Rathbone, *The Life and Correspondence of Field Marshal Sir D. Pollock*, London, 1873.

Macrory, Patrick, *Signal Catastrophe*, London, 1966.

Martineau, G.D., *Controller of Devils*, Lyme Regis.

Morag Murray Abdullah, *My Khyber Marriage*, London, 1990.

Pottinger, George, Lieutenant General, *Colin Mackenzie, A Story of the 1st Afghan War.*

Army Quarterly and Defence Journal, Vol 110, 3 July 1980.

Pottinger, George, *Twelve Indian Statesmen*, Edinburgh, 1883.

Sale, Lady Florentia, *The First Afghan War*, Patrick Macrory (ed.), London, 1969.

Sale, Lady, *Journal of the Disasters in Afghanistan*, London, 1843.

Shah Safia (ed.), *Afghan Caravan*, London, 1990.

Shahamar Ali, *The First Afghan War*, London, 1847.

Sirdar Ikbal Ali Shah, *Afghanistan of the Afghans*, London, 1928.

Skinner, A.M., *Sketch of the Military Services of Lt. General Skinner*, London, 1863.

Stubbs, F.W., *History of the Bengal Artillery*, London, 1887.

Trousdale (ed.), *The Gordon Creeds in Afghanistan*, London, 1984.

Trower, Lieutenant, F.G., *Manuscript Book*.

'Vincent Eyre and his wives' (*Journal of the Calcutta History Society*, Vol. V, 1915).

Warburton, Colonel Sir R., *Eighteen Years in the Khyber*, London, 1900.

Waller, N.H., *Beyond the Khyber Pass*, New York.

Also: An unpublished account of her family by Durani Warburton, and Letters and Information supplied by Mrs Sylvia Richardson, great niece of Shah Jehan Begum.

Glossary of Urdu and Afghan Words

Attah – Ground Wheat.
Barukzye – One of the five Durani tribes.
Cantonment – Barracks.
Char Chouk – Public Place.
Charpoys – Wooden beds with string foundations.
Cossid – Messenger.
Crore – 100 Lakhs of rupees (see Lakh).
Dahl – Pulse.
Doolie – Palanquin, usually used for carriage of the sick.
Durani – A ruling tribe of Afghanistan (literally 'Pearl' or 'Pearls').
Feringhee – European (Franks).
Ghee – Clarified Butter.
Jemadar – Of the same category but junior to subedar (see below).
Jezzail – A long-barrelled home-made musket, whose owners were known as 'Jezzailchees'.
Kafir – Infidel.
Kajawah – Pannier, used on camels.
Kote – Fort.
Kuzzilbash – Descendant of Persians.
Lakh – 100,000 Rupees.
Maund – 80lb of grain.
Mohur – Gold coin from India and Persia.
Moonshee – Interpreter or Secretary.
Nazir – Steward.
Palanquin – A form of doolie.
Pall – Kind of tent.
Pilau – Dish of Chicken with Rice.
Posteen – Sheepskin cloak with the fleece on.
Sepoy – Indian soldier.

Shah Bagh – King's garden.
Shyton – The Devil.
Sirdar – Chief.
Subedar – Senior Indian officer who did not hold an East India Company or Royal Commission, later known as a Viceroy's Commissioned Officer.
Yaboo – Afghan Pony.